Management Accounting in Support of Strategy

Management Accounting in Support of Strategy

How Management Accounting Can Aid the Strategic Management Process

Graham S. Pitcher

BUSINESS EXPERT PRESS

Management Accounting in Support of Strategy: How Management Accounting Can Aid the Strategic Management Process

First published in 2018 by
Business Expert Press, LLC
222 East 46th Street, New York, NY 10017
www.businessexpertpress.com

ISBN-13: 978-1-94784-381-3 (paperback)
ISBN-13: 978-1-94784-382-0 (e-book)

Business Expert Press Managerial Accounting Collection

Collection ISSN: 2152-7113 (print)
Collection ISSN: 2152-7121 (electronic)

Cover and interior design by Exeter Premedia Services Private Ltd., Chennai, India

First edition: 2018

10 9 8 7 6 5 4 3 2 1

Printed in the United States of America.

To Betty and Wilf

Abstract

During the 1980s and 1990s management accounting was criticized for being too operationally focused. The term strategic management accounting, as distinct from conventional management accounting, has been promoted as a means of addressing this criticism. There has, however, been considerable debate about whether strategic management accounting actually exists, and, if it does, what accounting techniques can be determined as strategic. This book takes a different approach in that it does not seek to categorize management accounting techniques, but takes the stance that management accounting is about providing information for managers to manage the business. The book explores how management accounting can support the strategic management process of analysis, formulation, implementation, evaluation, monitoring, and control.

The reader will gain an understanding of the strategic management framework, strategic models and tools, and how management accounting can support the strategic management process. It will be beneficial for undergraduate and postgraduate students studying strategy or management accounting. The book will also enable the practicing accountants to understand how they can make a significant contribution to the success of their organization by demonstrating how management accounting can be used in support of strategy.

Keywords

management accounting, management decision making, strategic management, strategic management accounting, strategy tool kit

Contents

Preface xi

Acknowledgments xiii

Chapter 1   Management Accounting and the Strategic
              Management Framework 1

Chapter 2   Understanding the Business Environment 15

Chapter 3   Internal Appraisal 35

Chapter 4   Corporate Appraisal 79

Chapter 5   Competitive Strategies 85

Chapter 6   Strategic Options Generation 103

Chapter 7   Strategic Evaluation and Choice 117

Chapter 8   Implementation Issues 133

Chapter 9   Multidimensional Performance Management 141

Chapter 10   Sustainability and Performance Management 169

Chapter 11   The Future Role of the Management Accountant 175

Appendix A: Strategic Management Accounting Techniques 179

Appendix B: Income Statement and Balance Sheet for X Inc. and Y Inc. 183

References 185

About the Author 189

Index 191

Preface

Management accounting is primarily about providing information for managers to enable them to manage the business. This includes supporting decision making at operational, business, and strategic levels within the organization. Many of the conventional accounting techniques are said to be too internally focused, primarily financial in nature, and best suited to supporting operational rather than strategic decision making. In the early 1980s authors began to suggest that accountants should look externally and provide information concerning competitors and markets. The term strategic management accounting was used to differentiate accounting techniques that focused on strategic aspects of the business from the more traditional tried and tested techniques. This prompted research into the adoption of strategic management accounting techniques, but still the term is not in common usage by practicing accountants, and the widespread use of strategic management accounting techniques is debatable.

This book takes a different perspective in that the strategic management process includes the analysis, formulation, implementation, evaluation, monitoring, and control of strategy, and that management accounting is able to contribute to each phase. A more recent movement of strategy as practice suggests that strategy is enacted by practitioners at many levels in the organization and is not the preserve of senior managers. It is possible to identify how every role in an organization contributes to the achievement of strategic objectives and therefore many operational decisions are actually more about enacting the strategy and contributing to the strategic management process in the area of implementation.

It was noted in a study undertaken by the author of this book that when making strategic decisions, such as the launch of new products or entering new markets, senior managers commented on "making sure that the margin was right." The margin, sales minus cost of sales, would not be considered a strategic management accounting technique, but it was clear that management accounting was being utilized to support the strategic decision. The focus of this book is therefore on how management accounting can support the strategic management process, regardless of whether the techniques are considered to fall under the category of conventional or strategic management accounting.

The structure of the book follows a strategic management framework set out in Chapter 1, and covers a range of strategic models and tools that can be used to develop strategy in organizations. It is important to state that decisions would not be based on the output of one strategic model or tool, but that the tools can, and should, be used together to provide a balanced view of the business. The focus, however, then turns toward how management accounting can support the various phases and draws out the financial aspects of using the various strategic models and tools in the strategic decision-making process. It has been said that finance is the language of strategy as strategic objectives are often communicated in financial terms. The view adopted in this book is that financial considerations are just part of the decision-making process and strategic decisions should not be made based on numbers alone, hence *Management Accounting in Support of Strategy.*

Acknowledgments

Thanks to the team at Business Expert press and all those involved for their support in the preparation of this book. I would also like to express my thanks to the Chartered Institute of Management Accountants' General Charitable Trust for funding the research project that gave me the idea to write a book about management accounting based around the strategic management process.

CHAPTER 1

Management Accounting and the Strategic Management Framework

What Is Management Accounting?

Traditionally management accounting has been distinguished from financial accounting by its focus on providing information for management activities. Definitions of management accounting in the 1970s encompassed activities such as providing support for managerial decision making, allocating resources, monitoring, and evaluating performance. Techniques such as budgeting and variance analysis to aid planning and control were commonplace, as were techniques such as investment appraisal and cost volume profit analysis. These techniques are still utilized today yet many of the traditional management accounting techniques and management information provided have been criticized over the years as being inappropriate for modern business. The information provided was typically internally generated and financial in nature, with a focus on accurately recording the cost of products, and monitoring performance via productivity and efficiency ratios. The principal criticism being that management accounting was focused on short-term operational decision making. There was a presumption that the accountant was merely the person with the numbers and the finance role was often devoiced from the development of strategy within the organization. Kaplan (1984) notably commented that management accounting should not be seen as a set of prescribed procedures and systems that could be applied universally, but that it should be tailored to serve the needs of the strategic objectives of the firm. Indeed, it is now understood that the management accounting system is contingent upon the organization's strategy, that is, there is not a one-size-fits-all accounting system.

During the 1980s and 1990s it was accepted that management accounting needed to develop to meet the changing requirements of business. As the business environment became more competitive, and the emphasis moved from long-range planning to strategic management, the call was not only for management accounting practices to respond to the changing needs of business, but also for accountants to become more involved in the strategic management process. This has been recognized in more recent definitions of management accounting. The Institute of Management Accountants (2008, p. 1) definition includes the phrases "partnering in management decision making" and "to assist management in the formulation and implementation of an organization's strategy." This indicates that the accountant is no longer seen as just the person with the numbers but is an active member of the management team involved in the strategic management process.

The Development of Strategic Management Accounting

During the 1980s and 1990s the concept of strategic management accounting emerged partly in response to the criticism that traditional management accounting was not serving the needs of strategic management. Various authors promoted aspects of information to aid strategy development. Simmonds (1981) focused his attention on the need for external information and in particular that which related to competitors and markets. Bromwich (1988) emphasized gathering and analyzing information pertaining to competitors and the benefits to customers over the long term; Govindarajan and Shank (1992) developed the concept of strategic cost management; Roslender and Hart (2003) focused on merging management accounting and marketing concepts within a strategic framework. Despite numerous offerings, a clear and agreed definition of strategic management accounting is yet to emerge from the published literature, but there is agreement that it involves providing information that supports strategic decision making. There has been a shift from providing information purely related to internal, quantitative, financial, past performance, and short-term decision making, to recognizing the need to include external, qualitative, nonfinancial, long-term, and future-oriented information.

Following the introduction of strategic management accounting to the literature a growing number of studies have been published that seek to ascertain the degree to which the new accounting techniques have been adopted in practice. A further difficulty, however, is that there is no definitive agreement on what constitutes a strategic management accounting technique. For example, Guilding, Cravens, and Tayles (2000) defined 12 techniques; Cadez (2006) defined 17 techniques; Cinquini and Tenucci (2007) defined 14 techniques; and Cadez and Guilding (2008) defined 16 techniques. A brief explanation of each technique is provided in Appendix A.

Various surveys over the past few decades have reported limited adoption and utilization of the defined strategic management accounting techniques and, although research suggests that practicing managers and accountants can see potential benefits in the use of the newer techniques, there is a tendency to prefer the tried and tested conventional management accounting techniques (McLellan 2014). More recent studies undertaken in specific industry sectors have indicated that some of the techniques ascribed to strategic management accounting are being adopted, for example, Oboh and Ajibolade (2017) in the Nigerian banking sector. However, it is still fair to say, as studies by Langfield-Smith (2008), Nixon and Burns (2012), and Pitcher (2015) have identified, that the term strategic management accounting has not as yet entered the lexicon of the accounting practitioner. These, and other studies do, however, find evidence that management accounting, whether conventional or strategic, is being used to aid strategic decisions and support the strategic management process.

Strategic Management

In the 1950s and 1960s management writers were discussing long-range planning. In many cases organizations were taking their annual budgets and extending them for a period of 5 to 10 years, thus creating a long-range plan. In the 1970s, and particularly in the 1980s, the focus shifted toward strategic planning as markets became more competitive. Toward the end of the 1980s and into the 1990s the focus changed again, this time toward strategic management, as organizations needed to become more responsive to changes in what was becoming a more dynamic and complex business environment. The original intension of strategic management accounting was that the information provided should aid strategic decision making and the strategic management process.

Here arises another difficulty—how to define the strategic management process. It is often described as a series of phases such as formulation, implementation, and evaluation of the strategy. A more encompassing and generally accepted definition is offered by Nixon and Burns (2012, p. 229) as containing the following key activities: "(1) development of a grand strategy, purpose or sense of direction, (2) formulation of strategic goals and plans to achieve them, (3) implementation of plans, and (4) monitoring, evaluation and corrective action." This portrays the process as a routinized and formal process, and although many firms still adopt a formal planning process it is also recognized that strategic decisions are often complex, nonlinear, and fragmented, and that the strategic management process is fluid and iterative in nature.

The Strategic Management Framework

Academic and practitioner texts discuss various methods, processes, and frameworks for the development of strategic plans. This section provides an outline of a strategic management framework (Figure 1.1). It is based

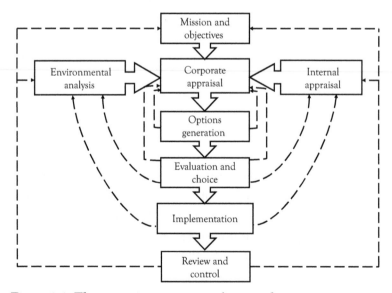

Figure 1.1 The strategic management framework

on the concept of a rational approach to strategic planning and forms a structure for the subsequent chapters. The explanation here is therefore deliberately brief as each element is discussed in detail later.

The framework incorporates key phases of analysis encompassing the external and internal analysis resulting in the corporate appraisal or SWOT (strengths, weaknesses, opportunities, and threats), the generation and evaluation of strategic options and strategic choice, followed by implementation, and finally the review, evaluation, and control of the current strategy. The dotted lines illustrate the iterative nature of the process.

Mission and Objectives

The mission is the rationale behind the business. It sets out the long-term aims and purpose of the organization as well as indicating the strategy, values, policies, and behavior standards. Organizations often develop a vision alongside the mission. This is usually broader, and shorter, than the mission statement and is often intended as a point of inspiration for employees to drive the business forward. It is common for organizations to promote their vision, mission, and the values that underpin these statements on their websites. This is extended for internal consumption to include the strategy and tactics, which creates a VMOST statement: vision, mission, objectives, strategy, and tactics. The objectives are more specific and set out what the organization aims to achieve. Ideally, they should be specific, measurable, agreed, realistic, and time bound (SMART).

Environmental Analysis

The environmental analysis is the subject of Chapter 2 and provides a means for identifying external factors that could affect an organization's ability to achieve its objectives. A strategic tool known as PESTEL (political, economic, sociocultural, technological, environmental, and legal) provides a framework that can be utilized to analyze changes in the general business environment. The focus of the analysis is on how the changes will impact on the industry and hence the organization. Models such as

Porter's Five Forces (Porter 1979) can aid the analysis at an industry level to identify the forces that will impact on the profitability and attractiveness of the industry, now and in the future. Competitor analysis is also a key area in this stage of analysis. Strategically the analysis helps to identify the opportunities and threats to the organization that are evident, or could emerge, from the business environment.

Internal Appraisal

The internal appraisal analyzes the organization's resource capability to achieve its objectives, given that environmental factors will impact on this ability. Various models can be utilized to aid the analysis, which are discussed in Chapter 3. These fit within a simple framework known as the 9 Ms: manpower, money, markets, machinery, materials, makeup, methods, management, and management information. These headings need to be viewed as pointing to broad areas requiring a detailed analysis. The analysis helps to identify strengths and weaknesses.

Corporate Appraisal

This pulls together the issues identified during the environmental analysis and internal appraisal and is the subject of Chapter 4. The environmental analysis is the source of opportunities and threats, while the internal appraisal is the source of strengths and weaknesses. However, during the environmental analysis it is not known whether a change creates an opportunity, or a threat, until this has been reviewed in light of the resource capability. It is not until the ability of the organization to deal with the change has been assessed that it emerges as an opportunity or a threat, hence the corporate appraisal provides the framework in which this can be identified. It is also worth noting that changes in the environment can provide an opportunity for some organizations while creating a threat for others, depending on the organization's ability to deal with the change. This has a strong connection to competitor analysis as strengths and weaknesses can be judged to be relative to competitors and a source of competitive advantage. Once identified, strategies can then be formulated that build on the strengths, address the weaknesses, grasp the opportunities, and minimize or avoid the threats, and that are consistent with the mission and objectives.

As part of the corporate appraisal a GAP analysis can be undertaken that ascertains the gap between an organization's stated objectives and the level of performance that will be achieved based on the current strategy, given the changes in the environment and its current resource position. If a gap is identified it requires the formulation and evaluation of strategic options to close the gap.

Options Generation

Strategic options can be considered under the heading of competitive strategy and methods of growth. During this phase the competitive strategy adopted by the organization can be assessed as to its appropriateness given the changes in the environment. Competitive strategies based on cost leadership and differentiation, as identified by Porter (1980), are discussed in Chapter 5. Options to generate growth include market penetration, consolidation, product and market development, and diversification. These are considered in Chapter 6, together with the methods of achieving organic and inorganic growth options, such as acquisition, merger, and joint development.

Evaluation and Choice

The various strategic options available to organizations need to be evaluated with respect to the resource capabilities and the ability to close any gap between stated objectives and forecast performance given the existing strategy. A framework such as suitability, acceptability, feasibility, and risk can be utilized to evaluate various strategic options, which would also include a financial evaluation. Suitability asks whether the strategy builds on the strengths, addresses the weaknesses, grasps the opportunities, and avoids or minimizes the threats. Acceptability reviews the strategy in relation to the stakeholders' expectations and interests. Feasibility reviews the practical aspects as well as financial evaluation, and risk assesses whether the proposed strategy is within the risk appetite of the organization. This can be remembered as a SAFeR evaluation and is considered in Chapter 7.

Strategic Implementation

Once the various strategic options have been evaluated and chosen it remains to be implemented. The strategy must be crystallized into operational budgets, targets, plans, and so on. This could also mean implementing changes to management information systems including the management accounting techniques utilized to support any changes in strategy. Management accounting support during implementation is discussed in Chapter 8.

Review and Control

This is the area where models such as the balanced scorecard can be utilized. Strategies are reviewed using a range of appropriate performance indicators that include nonfinancial as well as financial measures. Ultimately the review is considering how well the organization is meeting its objectives, which establishes the feedback loop to the start of the process. Part of the reason for any variation could be changes in the environment or resource capability, which illustrates the iterative nature of the strategic management process.

The traditional accountant would have focused attention on the review and control aspect of long-range and strategic planning. The strategic management process is more iterative and dynamic in nature. When an organization decides on a strategy and implements it successfully it can in turn impact on the competitive environment. In cases such as technology development it can impact on the general environment and change the cost structure of the industry, as in banking or retailing with the adoption of online business via the Internet. It is therefore important that the management accountant is willing and able to support management throughout the whole of the strategic management process. The aspect of performance management is considered in Chapter 9.

Who Sets the Strategy?

There is much debate in academic literature concerning who sets the strategy and who enacts strategy. There is a view that strategy is determined by management rather than being the sole preserve of the board of directors.

More recently strategy as practice has emerged as a school of thought that focuses attention on the activities and discourse of strategy formulation and enactment (Whittington 1996). The term strategizing has been promoted as a means of indicating that strategy is something that people do rather than describing a published plan or strategic intent. It is therefore worth remembering that it is people, rather than organizations, that make strategy. Strategy formulation can also be a social process and, in some instances, it may take on a political dimension. However, with that in mind, the term organization is used throughout the book when discussing strategy as the management accounting techniques considered can be utilized by people working at different levels within an organization and may also be of interest to not-for-profit organizations. Another important aspect to note is that the process depends on the organization and its organizational context, that is, it is not necessarily a case of one-size-fits-all. In today's business environment organizations need to be flexible and adaptable, which also extends to their strategic management process.

Formal Strategic Planning Versus Emergent Strategies

The process outlined so far gives the impression that strategic management involves a formal, linear process, albeit with elements of iteration and feedback. Mintzberg and Waters (1985) identified the concept of emergent strategies. Organizations articulate a planned and deliberate strategy that could either be realized or unrealized. However, targets such as sales or profits could be met, even though the intended strategy was not successful. This indicates that the management team should not focus solely on the outcome in terms of performance targets but need to understand why performance targets have been met or missed. For example, suppose the headline targets for sales and profits have been met, so on the face of it the strategy is working. However, when the sales data is analyzed in more detail it is found that the mix of products is different to that which was planned, the category of customer is different, and the main geographic location of sales is also different. This is an extreme example, however, on further analysis it appears that the actual strategy is not the reason why headline targets were met. It could be that a potential market of international sales is emerging to a different demographic, and this needs to be, in Mintzberg's terms, *crafted* into the future strategy of the organization. Emergent strategies can emerge based on a pattern of ad hoc decisions taken in response to a given situation, perhaps a competitor action, that when looked at in retrospect emerges as a potential strategy. They can also emerge based on what operational staff are doing. Perhaps the strategy is to spend heavily on marketing a certain type of product, but sales staff identify that other products are more in demand and push those at a local level, meeting sales targets, but not by the mix of sales initially planned. The natural inclination of management teams is to examine why strategies have not been achieved, but it is just as important to analyze the reasons as to why they have been achieved.

How Management Accounting Can Support the Strategic Management Process

Each chapter discusses the strategic models and frameworks and highlights how the accountant can contribute to the strategic management process. It is possible, however, to give a brief overview of how the accountants can contribute to the whole process rather than restricting themselves to the review and control activity.

- Mission and objectives
  The mission and objectives need articulating and crystallizing in quantifiable terms so that they can be measured. This could be a financial or nonfinancial measure. Many of the information systems that organizations have at their disposal can capture nonfinancial as well as financial data. Accountants are able to incorporate both aspects into management reports designed to evaluate the success of the current strategy. The reporting should not, however, focus solely on the explanation of past performance but on the impact of known events on future performance. For example, suppose an organization in the travel industry focuses on certain parts of the world where political unrest has affected sales for the first half of the year. The reporting should not only highlight the reason for the past performance being worse than expected, but report the

expected outcome for the full year taking into account the known changes in the business environment. This form of analysis and extrapolation can lead to the early identification of a strategic gap and, more importantly, the size of the potential gap.

- Environmental analysis
  The accountant can contribute to scenario planning by evaluating the potential financial impact of changes in the business environment as well as the more obvious monitoring of information of a financial nature, such as exchange rates, interest rates, and so on. It will always be a best estimate of the potential impact, often based on incomplete information. This can, however, help in determining the priorities of which environmental changes require more immediate attention and which can be placed on a watch list. Organizations cannot respond to every change in the environment, and close monitoring of the resource capability, particularly financial resources, can be an important part of the early warning system. Competitor analysis is also a key aspect of environmental analysis. The accountant is well placed to be able to contribute an analysis of the competitors' financial position as well as working with other functional colleagues, such as research and design, production, logistics specialists, and marketing teams, to ascertain as accurately as possible the cost structure of major competitors.

- Internal appraisal and corporate appraisal
  Contributions to the internal appraisal and corporate appraisal (SWOT) include the ascertainment of financial strengths and weaknesses and the determination of any profits gap, more importantly indicating how big the gap could become if no action is taken based on the balance of elements within the SWOT, for example, the incidence of significant weaknesses and threats. Also, analysis of supplier performance and customer profitability analysis, the profitability of the product portfolio and effectiveness of business processes, contribution to benchmarking for improvements, and assistance

in the analysis of the value system are all areas where the accountant is able to provide input.

- Options generation, evaluation and choice

  The accountant is able to contribute to the financial and strategic evaluation of strategic options. For example, by evaluating the long-term viability of competitive strategies, such as cost leadership, by monitoring the current profit margins and forecasting future profit margins. This can be important in a competitive market where competition is focused on price. Enhancing and maintaining a cost advantage via strategic cost management and activity-based management is another key area where the accountant can provide specific expertise. Accountants are also able to contribute to the maintenance of a differentiation strategy by undertaking competitor analysis and using the value chain to identify areas where value can be added to the product or service. Analyzing the relative profitability of different market segments can help to identify possibilities for organizations to pursue a focus strategy, which could be either a cost-focus or differentiation-focus strategy. Assisting in the evaluation of product development via techniques such as target costing, life cycle costing, quality costing, and pricing strategies provides opportunities for accountants to contribute to strategy development. Similarly, assisting in market development strategies by evaluating the potential profitability of entering new markets or exploiting new marketing channels can provide the management team with valuable information on which to base strategic decisions. A more obvious area where the accountant is able to contribute to the choice of strategic option is in the evaluation of the various methods that can be utilized to implement the chosen strategy, such as evaluating potential mergers and acquisitions, and the possibilities for joint development.

- Strategic implementation

  Crystallizing strategic plans into operational budgets is part of the implementation process, but also ensuring that the information systems can provide the information required to monitor and evaluate new strategies. All too often organizations fall victim to the reliance on legacy systems that are not capable of providing the information required to manage the business as it grows and develops. It is also important for the accountant to ensure that appropriate accounting techniques are utilized in supporting the organizational strategy. For example, the techniques that can be used to support a cost leadership strategy are different from those that will support a strategy of differentiation. It is equally important to ensure that appropriate reporting formats are used to help the organization understand the underlying causes of good, or poor, performance so that appropriate action can be taken.

- Review and control

  Implementation feeds into the review and control element that closes the loop to the mission and objectives. The accountant of 20 years ago would have been content to report on actual performance versus plan, but today's accountant would be involved in reporting on the effectiveness and continued viability into the future of the current strategy utilizing integrated performance measurement and highlighting any potential emergent strategies and the need for a strategic response to any potential profits gap.

CHAPTER 2

Understanding the Business Environment

The Changing Business Environment

The business environment of today is much more complex and dynamic than that faced by organizations 20 years ago. Factors such as developments in technology, communications, and transportation have contributed to the degree of globalization found in many industries. This can increase the degree of competition to which organizations are exposed creating the need to monitor existing competitors, and more significantly to be aware of potential competitors, that is, any product or service that a customer can use to fulfill the same needs as the organization's current offering. The information that organizations need to gather has broadened beyond the understanding of local markets. Technology has been a major driver for changes to industry structures, such as retailing and banking. The high street presence required by banks, in some cases, has become a liability, as fewer customers utilize the high-cost facilities. New competitors entered the market with a lower cost base, giving them a potential competitive advantage. Supply chains have become more complex requiring close monitoring of inter and intraorganizational collaborations. Consumers are becoming more sophisticated utilizing the technology to seek out the best deals, making customer retention and building loyalty more difficult. The need for organizations to understand the environment is becoming increasingly important, not just to identify the changes and to formulate appropriate responses, but to understand the drivers for change and, via the strategic decisions made, to be proactive and seek to manage the environment for competitive advantage.

Macro and Task Environment

The business environment can be viewed at various levels. Figure 2.1 illustrates the relationship between the macro, or general business environment, and the task environment.

The organization operates within an industry and therefore needs to monitor changes in the industry and assess the likely impact on the organization's ability to meet its objectives. It is important to note that changes in the industry will affect different organizations in different ways and therefore, in a competitive market, there is a need to assess how changes will impact on the organization in relation to its major competitors. In a similar way changes in the general environment, such as political influences, will affect some industries more than others, and therefore the organization needs to assess the impact on its industry and consequently on the organization itself. Part of the skill of environmental analysis is being able to evaluate which changes require a response and which do not. The most successful organizations develop the ability to evaluate the potential impact of changes and formulate a strategic response that provides a competitive advantage.

The task environment refers to specific elements of the environment with which the organization interacts more directly. This illustrates that

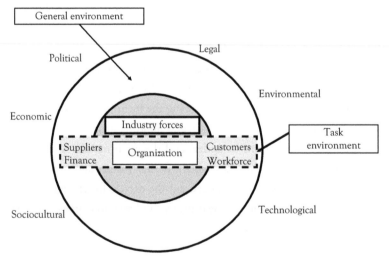

Figure 2.1 The business environment

suppliers and customers are factors within the environment, but that the organization interacts with these elements more directly. An organization also acquires its human resources and finance from the task environment, and therefore demographics, skills base, and factors affecting the organization's ability to finance its operations are of particular significance. The organization therefore needs to interact with its task environment, and those that can respond effectively to changes will perform much better than those that continue as if nothing has changed.

Why Undertake an Environmental Analysis?

Confirm or Invalidate Strategic Plans

Changes in the environment can invalidate or confirm existing strategic plans and influence whether organizations will meet their stated objectives. In some cases, it will require a change of strategy, or a realignment of objectives.

Identify Key Changes That May Affect the Industry

It is important that organizations understand the environment in order to ensure that they identify the changes that are occurring, or may occur, to the industry. The temptation might be to respond to every change. This can, however, create discontinuity within the organization and gives the impression of being reactive rather than proactive. To avoid this organizations need to be able to identify the key changes in the industry. This is where experience, knowledge, and intuitive understanding of the industry are useful and why some organizations get it right and others get it wrong, or more accurately why organizations adopt different strategies.

At one point the two major manufactures of airliners held different views as to how the future of air travel would develop. One believed hub and spoke would be the future, and the other believed point to point would be the preferred choice of passengers. Hub and spoke would require large aircraft to transport high volumes of passengers to the hub, which then transferred to smaller aircraft to reach their end destination.

The Airbus A380 was aimed at this particular market. Point to point required aircraft capable of flying long haul but with more fuel efficiency, and the Boeing 787 was aimed at this market.

Identify the Drivers for Change

It is not always just a case of identifying events in the environment as one occurrence does not necessarily imply a significant change. A series of events may develop into a trend that has more serious implications, but the key is to identify the drivers for change. This could have long-term implications for the structure of the industry and unless understood could leave the organization at a disadvantage.

For example, the Internet has enabled the development of new communication media and mobile devices are opening up many opportunities for marketing, purchasing habits, and new industries. However, linking this to the increasing use of social media by millennials and generation X gives a better understanding of how it can be used to grow existing markets and target new ones.

Identify the Differential Impact of Changes

The main focus of environmental analysis is about understanding how changes in the environment will impact on the organization and its ability to achieve the planned strategy, but it is just as important to identify the impact that the change may have on a major competitor compared to your organization. This recognizes the competitive nature of many markets and is known as the differential impact. Part of developing a competitive strategy is understanding how the competitors might respond to your strategy or their capability to respond to changes in the environment, a point we return to later in this chapter.

Understand the Likely Impact on Profitability of the Industry

Porter (1979) identified five forces that impacted on the profitability of an industry. These are the threat of new entrants, the bargaining power of suppliers, the bargaining power of buyers, the availability of substitute products and services, and the degree of competitive rivalry. It is important for organizations to understand how these forces are likely to impact on the profitability and, in some cases, the business model of the industry. For example, changes in technology may make it much easier to enter the industry, as has been seen in the banking sector. In some countries this was also coupled with changes in the regulatory environment for financial services. Linking these two events together could increase competition and reduce the overall profitability of the industry. These changes also impacted on the structure of the industry, and with it the cost base and the effective business model. Similarly, supermarkets and retailers that were late into the online shopping market fared less well than those that identified and responded to the trend more swiftly.

Identify Opportunities and Threats

Changes in the environment can create new opportunities or present new threats, as seen in the banking and retailing sectors with online shopping and transport systems where companies such as Uber have transformed the business model for taxi services. Not every organization will view changes in the environment in the same way. They may have different risk attitudes and therefore some will view changes as presenting opportunities, while others will see the same changes as threats. The organization's resource position can also have an impact on how changes are viewed, that is, the management team's ability to deal with the change. If an organization is in a very strong position changes may represent opportunities, but if in a relatively weak position the same changes could be seen as threats. Identifying the change and assessing the impact are part of developing a strategy.

The PESTEL Framework

The general or macro environment can be analyzed using a framework commonly referred to as PESTEL analysis. The acronym represents political, economic, sociocultural, technological, environmental, and legal factors. It is important to recognize that this is simply a framework to aid the thinking about the general environment. Often some elements will fit within more than one heading. For example, organizations within the travel business might see regulations around visas as legal or political. Factors such as foreign exchange rates affecting people's willingness to travel to certain locations could be an economic or political influence, as exchange rates are often influenced by government decisions as much as by economic factors. The idea is not to focus on how changes and influences are categorized as much as the fact that the change has been identified.

Political Factors

This heading can usefully include anything that emanates from a government policy, action, or influence. Typically factors identified here will be new elements of government legislation and policy, but this is not just limited to national governments. Many organizations will be affected by government decisions in other countries. Whether they operate in global markets, obtain supplies from overseas suppliers, or sell to selected overseas customers, the influence of government policy in other countries cannot be overlooked. This also extends to the general political stability of a region, or just uncertainty created by a potential change, or actual change in government. The impact of changes can be wide-ranging and affect more than one industry.

For example, the move by many governments to ban fossil fuel vehicles by a set date in the future does not only affect the motor industry. It will have wide-ranging impacts on the energy industry in terms of increased demand for electricity, battery technology, or alternative energy sources. It will also have on impact on the public or state sector transport industry, those involved in the provision of infrastructure, such as the provision of charging points, distribution companies, and many more. It is therefore important to think widely about each potential influence in the first instance. As already mentioned, organizations cannot respond to every change and therefore some form of prioritization needs to take place once the initial analysis has been completed.

Economic Factors

The economic cycle, whether economies are growing, in recession, or experiencing a period of transition, can have an impact on the industry and hence individual organizations. This is similar to the political factors in that it is not just national economies but global economies that could affect the organization.

A slowdown in car sales in one geographic area could influence a multinational car manufacturer, faced with excess global capacity, to close a car assembly plant in a different region due to employment laws that make it easier to shed labor in that country. This will impact on the local economy as employees lose their jobs, and may affect other smaller more local businesses. This illustrates that the interrelationships between PESTEL factors affect strategic decisions, in this instance, economic, political, and legal.

Changes in interest rates, inflation, and exchange rates can all affect businesses in different ways, therefore the organization needs to work through different scenarios to identify what the potential impact might be, if any, and adopt appropriate financial risk management strategies to manage the potential impact.

Sociocultural Factors

The most common element within the sociocultural heading is the changing demographic in many countries. This could not only be a threat to some industries, for example, an aging population may affect a manufacturer of children's games, but could also open up new opportunities or markets. For example, a developer and manufacturer of computer games targeted at children began to market a range of games targeted at older members of the population as "brain training." The selling point was that the aging customers could continue to exercise their brains to avoid dementia.

It is not only the consumer that is getting older but also the working population and the skill base. Watching trends in the skill base can provide useful information to organizations about potential issues that may develop in the future. Industries that rely on the STEM (science, technology, engineering, and mathematics) subjects may be concerned if students are not studying sciences, as this could flag up a potential issue with recruitment many years into the future. Therefore, the organization needs to begin to lobby government on education policy now, as well as promoting careers requiring the STEM subjects. It is as much about an early warning for the future as it is about immediate impacts.

National cultures and the emergence of different cultures with an increasing prominence in the world, as well as the changing mix of cultures in countries, have potential implications for products and services, the future customer base, and acceptability of working practices. Organizations must be aware of these changes to ensure that they remain current and are able to anticipate and plan for potential issues arising from these factors.

Consumers are becoming much less tolerant of poor behavior by organizations or practices that are deemed to exploit either labor or consumer groups. These trends, together with an increased awareness of sustainability issues, are pushing organizations toward a more responsible approach to business.

Technological Factors

Technology covers a wide range of areas and could include manufacturing technology as well as information and communications technology. Many production processes and office procedures have been automated and the use of artificial intelligence is constantly changing the way work is done and the skill set required. There are perhaps very few industries that have not been affected by the Internet and mobile technology.

The examples of banking and retailing illustrate how much technology has changed the structure and the business model of the industry, the products and services offered, and the way consumers interact with organizations, to highlight the importance of monitoring changes in technology and its potential impact. Using mobile apps to order a taxi or food is changing the way we interact with the controlling organization and intermediaries. Location trackers, as well as other "cookies," are changing the way organizations interact and market products and services to consumers. More recently there has been growing disquiet among consumer groups concerning the amount of personnel information that is held about individuals and the way that it is being exploited by organizations. The incidence of cybercrime also poses potential issues for organizations in the way customer information is handled as well as internal communications of a commercially sensitive nature.

Environmental Factors

The growing awareness of environmental and sustainability issues today means that organizations cannot ignore the potential impact that this element could have on the industry. As with technology, it is difficult to think of an industry that is not affected by sustainability and environmental factors. It can be seen in the product life cycle from "cradle to grave" or "cradle to cradle." It is not just in the initial product concept that sustainability needs to be taken into account, but in the use of the product and its disposal, including its potential to be recycled into another product, hence the "cradle to cradle" concept, where the technique of life cycle costing can be usefully applied to good effect.

Legal Factors

Legal issues tend to be new regulations that affect an industry, or changes in legislation. Health and safety issues fall within this area as well as issues such as patent and copyright protection. This would also include finance acts, taxation, and accounting rule changes where the accountants could put their particular expertise to good use.

Industry Analysis

Organizations operate within an industry and part of understanding the environment involves understanding the industry, as changes in the general environment can impact on different industries in different ways. Porter (1979) identified five forces that impact on the profitability and hence attractiveness of industries, and in turn help to shape the organization's strategy. The key, as with general environmental analysis, is not

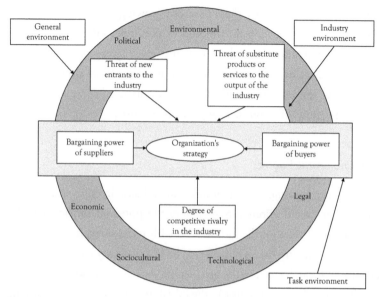

Figure 2.2 Industry forces impacting on an organization's strategy

simply to identify that something has changed but to be able to formulate a response to the change. Changes in the industry will have a more direct impact on an organization and could require a more direct response. Figure 2.2 illustrates the industry forces within the environment that could impact on an organization's strategy.

Threat of New Entrants or Barriers to Entry

The ease with which it is possible to enter an industry will impact on the degree of competition and potentially on the profitability of the participating organizations. If there are significant barriers to entry, such that the threat of new entrants is relatively low, existing participants may not compete so fiercely against each other. The stage of development that the industry has reached may impact on the degree of competition in that it is often easier to enter a new sector in which growth is high, as there is room in the market for new entrants. In more mature markets, where growth is low, it may be dominated by a few larger organizations making it more difficult to enter the market due to the power of the existing players. This of course ignores the argument that a lack of competition and high profitability of an industry may be seen as bad for the consumer and the government may take action to try and stimulate more competition, which reaffirms the need to monitor the general environment.

The banking industry demonstrates that technological changes can provide a means of getting over barriers to entry, that is, it is no longer necessary to have a strong high street presence, thus again illustrating the importance of understanding the implications of changes in the general environment and how they may impact on the industry. Typical barriers to entry could be the amount of capital investment required to enter an industry, the acquisition of necessary skills, the length of time for the experience curve to take effect, or the presence of existing strong brands synonymous with the product.

Bargaining Power of Suppliers

If the supply market to an industry is dominated by suppliers who are able to significantly control the supply or dictate terms to their customers, it will put upward pressure on the costs to the receiving industry. If the industry is not able to pass those costs on to their customers, this will impact on the profitably of the industry. In many cases organizations would seek to negotiate and agree terms with suppliers, which mitigates the supplier power. If one organization within the industry achieves this the competitors will seek to achieve the same ends, impacting on the degree of competition. This underpins the need to monitor the task environment and competitor responses to evaluate the potential impact on profitability.

Bargaining Power of Buyers

The bargaining power of buyers is similar to the bargaining power of suppliers, but in this case it is buyers who potentially have significant bargaining power that are able to exert downward pressure on the prices and hence profit margins. The cost of switching allegiance to another provider is significant here in that low switching costs, and in the case of many consumer markets, the volume of choice that consumers have, can increase the intensity of competition and hence impact on profitability.

Threat of Substitute Products or Services

It is important not to confuse the threat of substitute products or services with the threat from existing competitors in the industry. The heading of substitute products or services refers to the development of alternative ways that customers can use to meet their needs, which means they no longer need to buy the products or services supplied by the industry.

For example, in today's high technology environment video conferencing is a substitute for air travel, that is, it is not necessary to travel to a meeting, when it is possible to utilize a video conference or simply "Skype," or, at a more personal level, using WhatsApp or FaceTime. This is also an illustration of the need to think very widely about what customer needs the industry is fulfilling and hence of alternative means for fulfilling that need. For example, regional airlines are not just in the transport business, competing against road and rail transport, but also in the business of facilitating business meetings. Therefore video conferencing is a significant threat to regional airlines and indeed to international travel.

Rivalry Among Existing Competitors

The degree of competition in an industry will affect its profitability. The stage of the industry life cycle would also influence the degree of competition and to an extent how easy it is for new entrants to the industry to compete. For example, it is easier to enter and compete in a new and growing industry than it is to enter and compete in a mature industry where there are dominant players, which will aggressively defend their market share. Monitoring the degree of competition and competitors is also a significant element of environmental analysis, which is discussed in more detail later in this chapter.

Link Between Industries

Figure 2.3 illustrates that organizations, particularly those that operate in a business-to-business environment, need to extend their understanding of how the dynamics of the forces impact on their supplier and customer industries. Structural changes in supplier industries could impact on the

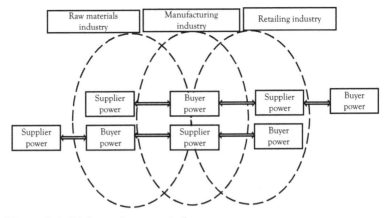

Figure 2.3 Linkages between industry sectors

resultant costs and possible relationships with suppliers, such as new entrants to the supply sector or substitute products or services that emerge. Similarly, for organizations operating in a business-to-business scenario a consolidation of industry players in the customer markets can potentially increase the bargaining power in the hands of buyers. The extended links between the suppliers and customers through the task environment indicate the need for good supply chain management, vendor analysis, and customer analysis discussed in Chapter 3.

Competitor Analysis

Undertaking competitor analysis is a useful activity in a competitive market, not just in terms of their product or service offering and prices, but in terms of understanding their future goals and strategy, as well as their strategic capability to deal with changes in the environment. Financial analysis can aid this process by identifying the financial strength or weakness of the competition, which can then be used in developing an organization's own strategy.

It is not just the existing competitors that need to be analyzed but also those organizations that could compete, that is, a competitor is any product or service that can fulfill the needs of the customer. This emphasizes the need to think widely about why customers buy the product or service.

Cluster Analysis

Strategy is as much about positioning the organization in the market as it is about being profitable. It is therefore possible for an organization to choose its competitors by choosing where in the market it positions itself, in effect choosing who it wishes to compete against. Positioning or cluster maps, illustrated in Figure 2.4, are useful in this respect, as they enable organizations to identify who the major competitors are, where in the market they have positioned themselves, and the basis of their competitive strategy.

The cluster analysis in Figure 2.4 indicates that there are two main competitors to A. It cannot, however, ignore D or E completely in case they change strategy and move closer to the middle ground. This analysis is also useful in identifying potential gaps in the market that might be commercially viable. It is possible to use any two axes to make comparisons. For example, in the PC market, price versus performance is often used; or in the retailing sector, service provision against price, or convenience against price. The choice of axes and making various comparisons against competitors by creating several cluster maps can provide insight into a potential competitive advantage that can be exploited and form the

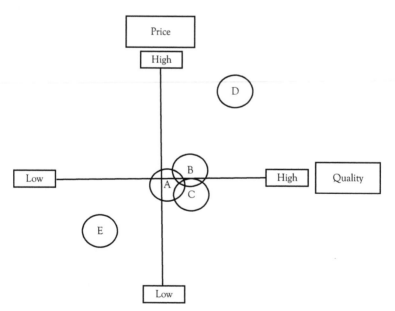

Figure 2.4 Cluster analysis for competitors

basis of marketing messages to differentiate the products or services from the competition.

Competitor Response Profile

An important aspect of competitor analysis that cannot be overlooked is the creation of a competitor response profile in which a profile is established over a period of time to monitor the response of the competitors to strategic decisions.

For example, knowing how long it takes a competitor to respond to new product launches, or their responses to changes in the pricing strategy can help with the formulation and choice of strategy adopted. In the case of new product launches this can indicate that competitors have a significant research and development capability and are able to respond quickly to new products. In the case of the pricing strategy, it could indicate that the competitors' cost base is similar and that they believe they have the margin to compete on price. Analyzing financial results as they are published will help to confirm overall levels of profitability in competitors and can confirm their ability to compete on price, and their ability to sustain the strategy into the future.

The key point about understanding a competitor's potential responses to strategic developments helps to understand the time frame or degree to which a competitive advantage can be enjoyed, or it may indicate the most likely strategic development to which the competitor will not, or is unable to, implement a speedy response.

Competitor Information

To undertake environmental and competitor analysis effectively, a system of data collection needs to be established. As an ad hoc exercise it can prove to be a costly and resource-intensive activity. However, if it is done on a regular basis, and monitoring systems are established with assigned responsibilities and mechanisms for dissemination of the information, it can be a manageable process.

According to Davidson, Keegan, and Brill (1997) sources of competitor information fall within three main areas: recorded information, observable information, and opportunistic information. Recorded information includes publicly available data such as the annual report and accounts, and investor reports; observable information includes experiencing the product or service, that is, visiting the shop, purchasing the product, or experiencing the service; opportunistic information includes talking to a key customer or supplier of a competitor at a trade conference. In some industries it is possible to reverse engineer the product.

For example, in the motor industry many manufacturers will purchase competitor products and test them under various conditions to record the performance, but they will also dismantle the product to understand its design and construction. This also provides information on the likely costs of production, as well as information about the customer requirements in different markets. The potential cost implications of safety regulations on the design of cars for different markets can also be ascertained. For example, the design requirements for the chassis are different in various countries. The more stringent the requirements are the greater the cost of meeting the standards. This raises an ethical dimension as to whether an organization adopts its own corporate standards in every market in which it competes, known as an integrity approach, or whether the organization adopts a compliance approach in which it meets the local requirements only. The cost implications of providing a chassis that meets higher safety standards could put the organization at a competitive disadvantage if competitors are only meeting the local, but lower, requirements. A cynical approach might suggest that there is no benefit in being more ethical than the competitors, unless there is a demand in the local market for a product, which meets higher safety standards than required by local laws, that is financially viable. This indicates that even when undertaking competitor analysis the environmental analysis cannot be ignored. For example, the legal element of PESTEL analysis is relevant here, as is the competitive rivalry element from the industry analysis. This illustrates that the models should not be used in isolation, but when used together they can help to form a good understanding of how the environmental factors impact on both the organization, and the relative position to its main competitors. Possible sources of competitor data are shown in Table 2.1.

Table 2.1 Typical sources of competitor information

Recorded data	Observable data	Opportunistic data
Annual reports and accounts	Pricing/price lists	Meetings with suppliers
Company websites	Product range, services offered	Meetings with common customers (e.g., those that dual source)
Press releases	Marketing campaigns	Trade shows
Newspaper articles	Specific promotional activity and advertising	Conferences
Analyst reports/investors section of company website	Public tenders	Sales contact meetings
Reports from regulatory bodies in the industry	Patent applications	Staff recruitment from competitors
Government reports	Reverse engineering the product	Discussion with shared distributors
Reports from organizations with an interest in monitoring corporate activity (e.g., pressure groups, consumer organizations)	Experiencing the service (e.g., mystery shopper)	Social contacts with competitors (e.g., family and friends)
Academic studies	Corporate activities of key personnel (e.g., public image of figurehead personality)	TV or radio discussion program (e.g., business or consumer affairs)

Management Accounting in Support of Environmental Analysis

The accountant is able to contribute to the environmental analysis aspect of the strategic management process in the following ways.

Evaluating the Potential Financial Impact of Environmental Changes on the Organization

The principle behind evaluating the potential impact of environmental changes on the organization is to facilitate a proactive response. An area where this can prove to be invaluable is where governments propose regulatory changes, or where a potential change in government could indicate a potential change in policy. The evaluation can provide the basis of a case for lobbying against such a change. It is more difficult to estimate the potential impact of changes in technology, or sociocultural shifts in domestic and global markets, and the evaluation inevitably involves estimates and "what if" scenarios, with a considerable number of informed guestimates in the initial stages. A case in point is BREXIT in the United Kingdom, where the decision to leave the European Union created considerable uncertainty for organizations in developing strategic plans, as the nature of the negotiations and the political dimension means that very little information emerges that can be relied upon with any degree of accuracy. This means that organizations need to monitor the situation closely and update their forward plans as information becomes available. As the outcome becomes more certain the initial estimates can be made more robust, and various scenarios investigated. In this way the organizations will be more prepared to implement specific strategies to deal with the final outcome once it is decided.

Evaluating Opportunities and Threats and the Strategies to Deal with Them

This is similar to evaluating the financial impact of changes but in this case the information available is more accurate and the likely outcomes can be evaluated with more certainty. The role of the accountant is to help management to understand the potential financial impact of various strategies. Scenario planning, by using a financial model of the business, can be used to estimate the potential impact of worst-case, best-case, and most likely scenarios. Maintaining the model, and making comparisons with actual results as strategies are implemented, can build up experience and understanding so that future impacts can be estimated with increasing levels of sophistication and confidence. This practice contributes to organizational learning in that future forecasting becomes more reliable as knowledge is built up of the impact of environmental changes on the achievement of various strategic responses.

Interpreting Environmental Data of a Financial Nature

Certain elements of the environment are financial in nature and the accountant can utilize this expertise to both capture and interpret the impact of data such as inflation, exchange rates, economic cycle, and commodity market prices that will affect the organization. Industry and media reports often carry data of a financial nature where accountants are able to assist in the interpretation and in understanding the potential impact on the organization.

Gathering Data for the Environmental Analysis Such As Competitor Analysis

The accountant is well placed to assess the financial strength of the key competitors and their ability to acquire resources to respond to changes. This contributes to building the competitor response profile and hence developing the organization's own strategic response.

Identifying Benchmarks on Performance of Key Players in the Industry

The accountant can assist in the identification, development, and monitoring of industry benchmarks. Competitor analysis can be a useful source of benchmarks to help to improve the performance of the organization or assess relative strengths and weaknesses.

Monitoring Internal Trends

The use of internal information should not be underestimated in environmental analysis. Internal trends may be an early indication of an environmental trend that has not yet been identified. For example, identifying that upward pressure on costs from suppliers may prompt an investigation to uncover the fact that purchasing managers are finding it more difficult to negotiate lower costs due to structural changes in the supply market. Or that marketing and sales staff are increasingly having to resort to sales discounts and promotions to encourage buyers to buy, which in turn puts pressure on margins, and may be indicative of the increasing choice and power in the hands of the buyers. Or that certain products are being purchased by a specific demographic group being indicative of a more general trend in the market that has not yet emerged from environmental data. Noting these trends and prompting investigations can often result in an early warning system for identifying the forces that are affecting the industry more generally. These can be helpful in developing a future strategy to deal with the changes and indeed to gain a competitive advantage.

CHAPTER 3

Internal Appraisal

Resource Audit

The internal appraisal is often referred to as a resource audit. It involves an assessment of the resources and capability of the organization and aids the identification of an organization's strengths and weaknesses.

The 9M's Framework

A common framework that can be utilized to aid a structured review of resources and capability is known as the 9M's framework.

- Men and women
- Management
- Money
- Makeup
- Machinery
- Methods
- Markets
- Material
- Management information

Men and Women

Men and women includes anything to do with human resources. It's not just about how many people are employed, but whether they have the right skill set and experience. It raises questions such as, are the recruitment and retention strategies working? Is the organization undertaking sufficient staff development to keep the skill base current and staff motivated? It is important to bear in mind that an organization obtains its human resources from its task environment so there is a strong link between the resources and environmental trends. Certain industries require certain skills.

A key message is that the internal analysis is not undertaken in isolation and is not just about assessing the current capability, but assessing the supply of, and the ability to acquire, future resources. As with most resources, their acquisition involves financial aspects where the accountant can provide expertise and assistance to the HR professional to evaluate potential strategies, such as changes to the pay and benefits package within the organization and assessing the overall impact on profitability. It is accepted that in large organizations the HR professionals will be equipped with this expertise, but the accountant is a valuable resource and has the overview of the financial situation that other functional specialists may not have.

Management

The element of management is not just whether the organization has a management team, but does the organization have an appropriate management structure, that is, is it centralized or decentralized and is that appropriate? Linking this to human resources (men and women) a review of the skill base within the senior management team can be included to ascertain whether the management has the correct skill set or mix of skills to cope with future strategies.

Money

Money is not just about how much money the organization has now, but the organization's ability to raise sufficient finance in the future to finance the chosen strategy, that is, what does the balance sheet look like, current levels of gearing, assets for security, and so on. This also serves to illustrate that elements of the 9Ms framework are not to be viewed in isolation as the asset base, considered under the heading of machinery, can have an impact on the future finances. For example, assets can be used as a source of security for a loan, or alternatively can create the need for additional finance to replace aging assets.

Makeup

Makeup refers to the organization's structure and culture. The question being posed relates to whether the organization has the right structure and culture to implement successfully the chosen strategy, given the changes in the environment? For example, a more dynamic and complex environment may require a shift to a more flexible and decentralized organization structure, granting autonomy to business units in order to facilitate speedy responses to competitor actions.

Machinery

The heading of machinery refers to all assets and includes reviewing aspects such as the age of assets and whether the organization has the finance available to replace them when required. Reviewing whether the technology being utilized is up-to-date or is it putting the organization at a disadvantage? The asset value can also be considered under this heading with a strong link to the element of money. For example, organizations in high street retailing or property management would be interested in what is happening to the value of the asset base.

Methods

Methods refers to the way of working and asks questions such as, could things be done more efficiently and more effectively? This could include manufacturing, design, administration, and customer service—in fact any activity undertaken by an organization. Techniques such as benchmarking (see Chapter 9) or analysis of the value creation system, considered later in this chapter, could be utilized to explore if the organization's performance can be improved.

Markets

The markets heading facilitates a review of the markets in which the organization currently operates or is planning to enter. This could mean withdrawing from markets as well as expanding in to new markets. Portfolio analysis, such as the Boston Consulting Group matrix, considered later in this chapter, can be utilized to help review the product portfolio and the markets in which the organization operates. This aids the development of strategies to manage the balance of the portfolio and the relative competitive position. The product life cycle, also considered later in this chapter, is a useful tool as organizations need to assess where products are within their life cycle, which again illustrates the link to the environmental analysis as changing social trends (a change from voice to text communications) and political (governments setting targets to ban the sale of fossil fuel vehicles), legal (increased fire resistance standards on building materials), and environmental (increased pressure from consumer groups to enhance the recyclability of products) factors potentially impact on the product mix and product life cycle. Customer analysis can be considered under this heading and is dealt with later in the chapter. Not all customers provide the same level of profitability due to the different demands placed on the organizations resources, which results in different levels of "costs to serve." At a simple level retailing organizations can analyze the profitability of online versus in-store customers.

Material

The materials heading includes an evaluation of supplier relationships as well as changes in the materials that are used. Aspects such as reliability, quality, cost, and location relative to supply can be evaluated. Do current suppliers have the capacity to grow with the organization? If not, then alternative suppliers need to be sought or the possibility of dual sourcing needs to be considered.

Management Information

The heading of management information encompasses reviewing the capability of the systems to provide the information to managers required to manage the business effectively and to develop, implement, evaluate, and monitor strategy. Many organizations find that they are still relying on the information systems and technology installed 10 years ago but that the business has changed. Consequently, the managers do not have access to the information they need to run the business as it is now. Information systems develop entropy over time and become less useful, unless the information provided keeps pace with the business as it grows, develops, and changes in response to the environment. Legacy systems, including the financial systems, have developed in a piecemeal fashion, often by implementing workarounds in order to cope, only to find that the lack of integration creates inefficiencies such that the cost of providing information becomes expensive or prohibitive.

Portfolio Analysis—The Boston Consulting Group Matrix

The Boston Consulting Group (BCG) developed a matrix that assesses an organization's products in terms of cash generation and cash expenditure requirements. The products are categorized in terms of market growth rate and relative market share. The analysis falls within the range of strategic tools that are used in portfolio analysis. The portfolio analysis matrix shown in Figure 3.1 can be used to analyze an organization's portfolio of products, or in the case of a conglomerate organization that comprises of many different businesses, or business units, the model can be used at a corporate level, that is, managing a portfolio of businesses.

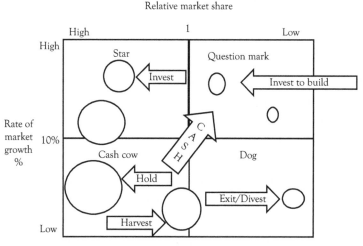

Figure 3.1 The portfolio analysis (BCG) matrix

The Axes

The rate of market growth can be calculated by using the formula:

$$\frac{\text{Market sales this year} - \text{Market sales last year}}{\text{Market sales last year}} \times 100 = \%$$

The obvious difficulty can be in identifying accurately the value of the market sales. This could be obtained from external sources, but it is not always possible to identify the total market. The assessment also depends on how the market is defined, for example, is it the local market, is it the national market, is it the global market, or is it a segment of the total market? (e.g., the market for accountancy training or a broader market such as business education). This is one of the difficulties of the portfolio model, or indeed most strategic analysis tools, in that it is not a precise science, hence best estimates often need to be utilized. It is possible to use the organization's own sales as a proxy for market sales in order to obtain an estimate of the likely growth in the overall market. This assumes that the organization's sales are growing at the same rate as the market, but in the absence of any better information is probably good enough. The mid-point of the rate of market growth axis is typically denoted as 10 percent, that is, greater than 10 percent is high growth, and below 10 percent is low growth.

Relative market share is assessed as a ratio. It is the market share of the organization compared with the market share of the largest (or nearest) competitor and is assessed on a logarithmic scale. The Boston Consulting Group chose to utilize market share as a way of estimating the costs associated with given products. The rationale for this is that both costs and market share are connected with production experience, as experience in satisfying a particular market demand increases, market share can be expected to increase and costs to fall, due to the effects of the experience curve. However, as already mentioned, defining the market can be a subjective process. It also presumes that the market size can be estimated with some degree of accuracy. This is not always possible and therefore the actual position of a product within the matrix can be a subjective opinion rather than a definitive outcome. The key point here is that if the assessments for products are undertaken consistently then a reasonable representative of the product portfolio can be achieved. The relative market share is calculated as follows:

$$\frac{\text{Market share (or sales value) of organizations's product}}{\text{Market share (or sales value) of nearest competitor's product}}$$

Generally the midpoint of the relative market share axis can be denoted by the number one, that is, unity. Therefore, if the relative market share is greater than one it has a relatively high market share (and is probably the market leader) and, if lower than one, a relatively low market share.

Categorization and Balanced Portfolio

The products or business units are categorized as question marks, rising stars (or just stars), cash cows, and dogs. The question marks are cash using as the organization tries to grow the market share, with rising stars still requiring investment to match the growth in the market. As the market growth slows, and if market share is retained, the cash cows provide the cash for investment in question marks and rising stars, with dogs potentially becoming a drain on cash resources. The ideal situation for an organization is to maintain a balanced portfolio of products. Each circle shown in Figure 3.1 represents a product, the size of which represents the proportion of total sales. It can be seen that ideally the cash cows are the largest proportion of total sales with question marks and dogs representing much smaller proportions.

Strategies That Can Be Employed

There are four main strategies than can be employed with respect to products, market segments, or business units.

Build/Invest

A build strategy, as the label suggests, attempts to build the market share, which requires investment in marketing and resources. A key factor is the ability to meet increased demand as the market and market share grow. This is most appropriate for products and divisions that fall into the category of question marks. The market potential needs to be assessed in order to decide on the specific marketing strategy as there is no guarantee that the product will be successful. Where there are several question mark products a decision needs to be made as to how to prioritize investments between the products based on their market potential. Products in the question mark category are generally cash using and carry a high business risk.

The strategy is also appropriate for products and divisions in the star category. In the short term, these require investment in excess of the cash they generate, in order to maintain their market position, but promise high returns in the future. The strategy would be to continue to build the market share. The market is still growing at this point and therefore it is important to continue the investment in the product. If investment is cut back the danger is that competitors will capture the growth in the market and the market share will reduce, with the result that the product falls back toward the question mark position.

Hold

A hold strategy, as the label suggests, seeks to maintain the current market position. This involves encouraging repeat purchases, maintaining customer loyalty, and maximizing contribution per product. This is typically applied to the category of cash cows and the cash generated is invested in question marks and rising stars.

Harvest

A harvest strategy seeks short-term earnings and profits at the expense of long-term development. This often involves a discounting or promotional policy to maximize sales revenue. Utilizing a farming analogy indicates that if a product is harvested it requires a new product to replace it. This is often appropriate for end-of-line products that are being replaced by a new model.

Divest

Divestment reduces negative cash flow and releases resources for use elsewhere. It is typically considered for products falling into the category of dogs. The choice here is to divest the product in some way. It need not be that the product is discontinued altogether. There may be occasions where it can be sold to another company under license so that there is no additional investment required, but a royalty is still received providing a limited amount of income. It may also be possible to find a niche market where the product can extend its life cycle.

Uses of Portfolio Analysis

Balanced Portfolio

The prime objective is to achieve a balanced portfolio, that is, to ensure that the company has new products that are capable of replacing the old products as they begin to lose their market appeal or technology begins to make them obsolete. This emphasizes the importance of monitoring the environment, particularly the competitive environment, and evaluating the potential impact of changes on the profitability and cash generation properties of product combinations.

Assess Trends Over Time

Portfolio analysis can be used to assess trends over time to monitor the impact of the strategies being adopted. For example, are the question marks turning into stars? What is happening to the market growth rate? Have the stars maintained the market share to become cash cows?

Assessing the Potential of Strategies Within the Portfolio

The analysis can be used to test the risk of various strategies by undertaking scenario analysis, or a "what happens if?" style of analysis, to test the impact on the overall balance of a portfolio if certain strategies are adopted for different products or business units. Utilized over time this can encourage organizational learning as the impact of various strategies is monitored and evaluated.

Competitor Analysis

Information about the competitors' products and market share needs to be gathered as part of the analysis, which makes it possible to utilize portfolio analysis as part of competitor analysis, that is, to gain an understanding of the strength of a competitor's portfolio of products. This can help to formulate an organization's own strategy, which makes portfolio analysis a useful tool to monitor potential competitors via trend analysis, as small competitors can often grow quickly to pose a significant threat.

Potential Drawbacks of Using Portfolio Analysis

As with all models and frameworks it is important to note that running a business is not necessarily a precise science and that care needs to be exercised when interpreting the information provided by the models. Just as decisions should never be taken based purely on the numbers, decisions should never be taken based on using one model in isolation.

Possible Synergies Between Products

There is the potential to miss possible synergies between products. Consideration needs to be taken for the existence of complementary and substitute products within the portfolio when formulating strategy. This can impact on the timing of product launches and withdrawals from the market. Scenario analysis and experience aid the strategic decision-making process, emphasizing the need to monitor the mix of products, and purchases of product combinations, on a regular basis.

An Underlying Assumption That High Market Share Is Always Good

Assuming that achieving high market share is the ultimate aim can send the wrong message to nonfinancially aware managers who may push sales at any cost rather than sales to profitable customers. Also high market share does not necessarily lead to high profits as markets can be very competitive with low margins. Similarly it could be that it is possible to make a reasonable profit from a small market share. It is also worth remembering that market share is not the only indicator of success.

High Volumes of Data Required

A potential drawback is the requirement for information about market share and competitors' products. If an organization has a large volume of products it requires high volumes of data to be collected. For this reason it is often only practical to undertake the analysis for key brands. However, the use of technology and external information that is available in electronic format can help alleviate the information overhead.

Financial Controls and Accounting Techniques

The financial controls and accounting techniques that are appropriate for each category of product can be linked to the critical success factor of each stage.

Question Marks

The critical success factor for products in the question mark category is to successfully develop and launch new products into the market. This requires investment in new product development, the control of that investment, and the evaluation and approval of the business case for new products. Investment appraisal techniques (see Chapter 7) are a key part of the business case and evaluation phase. The investment appraisal included within the plan will not only include targets for the initial investment in operational capability, but also marketing spend, sales, costs to serve, and time frames for key stages. As well as being involved in monitoring the success of the product launch the accountant will have been involved prior to this in evaluating the viability of the product at the development stage. This may have included the use of techniques such as target costing and life cycle costing, as well as strategic pricing. Activity-based costing (ABC) may be utilized in order to establish the cost of a product in relation to pricing strategies, or as part of target costing exercise to ensure sufficient margin is made. These techniques are discussed in Chapters 5 and 6.

Rising Stars

As the product moves to the star category the critical success factor is growing the market share. The concept of investment appraisal is still highly relevant at this stage as further investments in marketing are made to grow the market share. The focus of the marketing spend switches from awareness advertising to building brand loyalty. The experience curve will begin to impact on costs as market share rises, therefore the impact of costs needs to be carefully monitored. While ABC may have been utilized at the question mark stage, as the volume grows more accurate data becomes available in order to estimate future activity levels, ABC becomes more relevant in helping to identify areas for improvements and where the costs of activities can be reduced. This can also be undertaken in conjunction with the analysis of the value creation system, discussed later in this chapter. The impact of promotional activity on margins needs careful monitoring to ensure that it does not jeopardize the future viability of the product by creating a perceived level of pricing that is not viable in the long term. Competitive responses also require monitoring in order to retain the market share. At this stage it is important not to revert to a reactive strategy but to continue to evaluate the potential impact of increased investment on future viability of the product and to maintain the balance of the portfolio. The potential impact of investment in one product on the balance of the portfolio could be considered via scenario analysis.

Cash Cows

The critical success factor of the cash cow category is to maintain the market share and margins. Here we are expecting a return on the total investment made to enable the product to achieve the dominant position in the market. The importance of maintaining the contribution per product and customer profitability take on more significance at this stage.

Dogs

At the dog stage the critical success factor becomes minimizing the cost base with an emphasis on freeing up cash flow to invest resources in other products. The potential to find niche markets where the product could still provide a positive cash flow should also be investigated.

The Case of Nokia

In 2008 Nokia was a leading manufacturer of mobile phone handsets and network infrastructure provision. The company operated within three divisions: Devices and Services, Here (digital mapping/location), and Nokia Siemens Networks (the provision of network infrastructure). In the Devices division Nokia's phone lost market share as the development of the smartphone became the consumer preference. In an attempt to compete with the smartphone, Nokia developed the Lumia range of products, which linked up with Microsoft to use the Windows Phone 8 operating system. The basic premise was that, as many consumers used a Microsoft operating system on their computers, linking it to the phone would be an attractive offering. Nokia attempted to compete with the established smartphone providers by launching the Lumia 1020, which was described by reviewers as a digital camera with some phone features built in. However, this was not as successful as Nokia had hoped and the Devices division began to lose money and market share continued to decline. The Network division was also seeing its markets becoming more competitive and, although still profitable, Nokia's sales had been relatively flat causing a decline in market share. The Here division was the only division to show signs of growth in both sales and profits. The movement in their product portfolio between 2008 and 2013 could be represented as shown in Figure 3.2.

Nokia reviewed its strategy and identified that its key strengths were technology development, brand recognition, and experience of the telecoms market. They sold the mobile devices business to Microsoft mobile and focused on the provision of network infrastructure and its digital mapping business. The company was restructured into two divisions to take advantage of its key strengths—a Networks division and an Innovation

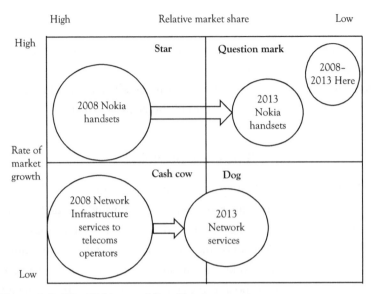

Figure 3.2 The Nokia portfolio of business units

division, which included digital mapping. They purchased Alcatel-Lucent to strengthen its digital mapping business and have entered the market for virtual reality and digital health, building on its strengths in technology and innovation. A few years after this Nokia re-entered the mobile market with a company called HMD-Global to build on the Nokia brand name. Whether this was a good move remains to be seen.

Product Life Cycle

The product life cycle (PLC) is a commonly referred to model and represents the life of a typical product from initial launch to eventual decline. The representation that is often referred to includes four stages of the sales life cycle: introduction, growth, maturity, and decline. The representation in Figure 3.3 brings in an element of the market life cycle to include the shakeout phase. Typically as a market develops and shows signs of profitability it attracts new entrants, but as the market growth slows the weaker competitors get shaken out of the market, often due to a lack of resources to match the growth, or the inability to gain sufficient market share to enjoy economics of scale. This can lead to the mature stage being dominated by a few large organizations.

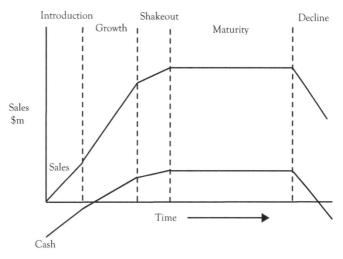

Figure 3.3 The sales and market life cycle

The representation in Figure 3.3 includes a second line to represent cash, which can also be indicative of profit. This illustrates that at the introduction stage, due to increased marketing expenditure and low sales, not to mention the development costs, the product is using, rather than generating cash (or making a loss). As the product sales grow, and marketing changes from awareness advertising to building up brand loyalty, the product begins to generate a positive cash flow (or profit). Once the product reaches maturity it is generating positive cash flows and profits, which decline as the product becomes out of date or loses its market appeal and sales volumes decline.

Based on this explanation of the PLC and the pattern of cash usage/generation the four main stages can be equated to the portfolio analysis. Introduction equates to question marks; growth equates to stars; maturity equates to cash cows; decline equates to dogs. It does not, however, mean that all products follow the same pattern. Picturing the PLC along with portfolio analysis does help to illustrate graphically that when products are denoted as stars the market is still growing, and therefore the investment in the product and marketing is still required. Linking the two models together also helps to illustrate that the organization does not want to wait until a product moves into decline before thinking about a replacement.

The Accountant and the PLC

The financial control measures noted under portfolio analysis are applicable with the PLC. However, the PLC enables other key strategic aspects to be considered where the accountant is able to make a contribution.

Production Pattern and Inventory Decisions

Once a product has been developed and the market testing carried out (if applicable) the organization has a decision to make as to the inventory and production pattern with its related impact on finance and cost. If the product is marketed in such a way that the anticipated sales upon launch will be high, then a significant volume of products might need to be manufactured in preparation for the launch. If the product does not sell well then there will be a high inventory level taking up space and tying up capital, which might have to be scrapped and written off if not sold. An alternative approach might be to gear up for very flexible manufacturing such that replacement inventory can be manufactured at short notice to satisfy demand. The decision here is crucial as there is nothing worse than creating demand for a product that is satisfied by a competitor, because the organization cannot satisfy the demand it has generated. The accountant needs to work very closely with marketing and production staff in order to ensure that the costs and benefits of various strategies are understood. The same is true for the provision of a new service in that the resourcing decision related to the provision of skills to meet growth in the market is just as significant, that is, it may take time to recruit sufficient staff to deal with a surge in demand, during which time sales are being lost.

Pricing Decisions

The pricing decision is also key as to whether to go for a high price associated with market skimming or a low price targeted at market penetration (see Chapter 6). Choosing a pricing strategy that can be maintained throughout the product's life, allowing for promotional adjustments from time to time, can be critical in positioning the product in the market as well as the long-term viability of the product. Maximizing and maintaining the contribution per product can be key to the cash generation and profitability of the product as volume increases and average cost per unit reduces. Understanding the dynamics of this in a specific market can feed into future product developments and target costing analysis as experience of the cost behavior linked to marketing strategy is gained through monitoring product launches over time. As organizations begin to develop a better understanding of the cost behavior of the organization and the market sector, this can be applied to competitor analysis and competitor costs can be estimated with a higher degree of certainty.

Cost Implications of Competitive Strategy

The level of competition and structure of the market can also change as the product/market life cycle progresses, requiring a review of the strategy. For example, in the early stages of the product life cycle competition is often based on price. The initial product, such as the mobile phone, is often fairly basic (e.g., the early mobile phones made telephone calls) and once the first one is launched competitors copy the concept and produce similar products with much the same functionality. As the product moves through growth to maturity and the market price ranges are established, competition tends to move away from price toward product differentiation, that is, mobile phones are developed with different features and functionality. For example, new features such as cameras are added such that the fact that they make telephone calls is now incidental to the purchasing decision. The development of products for different segments of the market becomes more relevant, for example, mobile phones targeted at teenage boys with ease of online game playing, or those targeted at the business market with personal organizers and other functionality useful for the busy executives. This is linked to the process of fragmentation as product variations are targeted at specific segments of the market. The cost base changes due to the loss of some economies of scale that were achieved from the production of a single standard product. When a range of product variations are required the economies of scale can be lost causing the cost base to rise. Deliberately fragmenting the market is a potential strategy for competing against a cost leader. This can sometimes allow smaller players to enter the market by targeting a single segment assuming that there is sufficient volume. This is discussed in more detail under competitive strategies in Chapter 5.

Customers

It is often said that the customer is the most important stakeholder in any business. In business-to-business situations this is still true, but the concept can be extended through to the end consumer such that the most important stakeholder is the customer's customer, that is, the ultimate consumer or beneficiary. It is generally agreed that customers should be the key focus for management in that products and services should provide what the customer wants. There is naturally a close link to market research in identifying the customer needs and the accountant can play a key role in assisting in the analysis of establishing the most profitable way of satisfying those needs.

Many organizations, especially small- to medium-sized organizations in business-to-business markets, sell to a relatively small number of customers, and some of these may be designated key accounts, that is, those customers on which they depend to a larger degree than others. Often the key account customers can be the reason why other customers buy or access the organization's products or services. This may make some customers more strategic than others.

Due to the different demands placed on an organization's resources by different customers or customer groups, not all customers generate the same level of profit. Indeed some may be unprofitable. Customer analysis includes looking at different aspects associated with meeting the needs of customers in a way that is mutually beneficial to both customer and the organization. The analysis seeks to establish who the good customers are and who the bad customers are. Ideally the company wants to retain the profitable customers and lose, or reduce, the nonprofitable ones. However, it is a marketing-led strategy that achieves this. It is not good public relations to say to one group of customers they are not wanted, but organizations can change the focus of the marketing so that they don't attract the unprofitable customers.

Understanding Customers

The following factors enable a good understanding of customers and their potential to generate profit for the organization.

Customer Identity

Identifying the customer is easier in business-to-business markets than in retail markets, but understanding who the customers are in terms of the status in the market place, the products they make or sell, and size and potential for growth can be useful in establishing their potential for the organization. The use of loyalty cards helps understand consumer buying behaviors in retail markets.

Customer History

Customer history is important in terms of volume of purchases, ordering patterns such as regular or ad hoc, and how long they have been a customer. These factors can help to identify the loyal customers.

The Relationship of the Customer to the Product and to the Potential Market

It is important to understand the relationship of the customer to the product. For example, what does the customer do with the product? Is it a component part of their final product and, if so, how important is it and how many other organizations can supply it? If a customer is a key player in their market other organizations may opt to follow their lead and purchase the product or service. Thus the customer becomes a strategic customer and significant for attracting other potential customers.

Customer Attitudes and Behavior

Some customers can be very demanding while others are less so. Demanding customers can be useful in driving improvements in both product and service levels but can also make these unprofitable if the costs to serve become prohibitive. The strategic importance of the customer to the organization in terms of the relationship to the potential market will impact on the willingness to satisfy the demanding customers.

The Financial Performance of the Customer

Customers that are growing and very successful are likely to continue to be in business and generate future business. The payment record is also relevant here as this will impact on the working capital cycle and the cost of financing different customers.

Customer Profitability Analysis (CPA)

The profit earned from each customer is not necessarily the same, as different customers can make different demands on the company resources, which means that the costs to serve each customer, or customer group, could be different. It is often said that the Pareto analysis, or 80/20 rule, applies in that 80 percent of the organization's profit is generated from 20 percent of the organization's customers. This also means that 80 percent of the firm's customers are only generating 20 percent of the profit. In fact some customers may even be generating losses when the costs of servicing them are deducted from the sales revenue that they generate.

It may not be possible to analyze revenues and costs to each customer in every industry, but it may be possible to categorize customers and analyze sales and costs to customer groups or categories. For example, a company may sell computers to businesses and also individuals. There may be some business customers that are large and designated key accounts, where a member of the sales team is dedicated to servicing their needs, and therefore the costs of the sales personnel can be allocated directly as a cost to serve that customer. However, the cost of a single sale to the private individual instore will be more difficult to analyze directly to the specific customer but it may be possible to separate out certain costs associated with servicing the sales to private individuals who purchase in-store and those who purchase online. An organization may decide to focus on selling to businesses or to private individuals as a result of analyzing the costs associated with supplying both markets. The decision, however, should not be made based solely on the numbers. There may be some synergies and cross fertilization between the two types, for example, it may be that on closer examination one of the reasons why private individuals buy from the organization is because the organization for which they work is a customer.

Benefits of Customer Profitability Analysis

Customer profitability analysis (CPA) focuses on profits generated by customers and suggests that profit does not automatically increase with sales revenue. CPA can benefit a company in the following ways.

Identify the Most Profitable Customers

CPA enables a company to identify the most profitable customers or customer groups and therefore to focus resources. In some instances it may indicate that it is worth making organizational changes to facilitate certain customers. This could range from establishing a warehouse close to key customers or markets to establishing strategic business units to service specific market segments.

Development of Marketing Strategies

By identifying the profitable customers or customer groups CPA aids the development of marketing strategies to target the acquisition of profitable customers and to adopt strategies to discourage the unprofitable customers. This could be as simple as setting a minimum order quantity or charging for delivery on orders below a certain value. This passes on some of the costs to customers.

Level of Service or Onward Charging to Customer

Decisions as to the level of service provided, or functionality required by customers. It may be that demanding customers are unprofitable due to changes required in the standard product. Understanding the relative profitably of the customer base can aid the decision as to whether to charge a higher premium for changes or additional levels of customer service.

This has to be balanced with the strategic importance of the customer to the organization in that it may be that other more profitably customers are attracted to the organization because of the key customer. The overall impact on profitability of losing the key customer can be evaluated.

Understanding the Financial Boundaries in Negotiations

Understanding the financial impact of losing key accounts can aid negotiations as the organization has a better understanding of the limits within which it can negotiate a profitable relationship with the customer, or even knowing when to walk away.

Financial Impact of Changes to Customer Mix

Understanding CPA helps quantify the financial impact of proposed changes to the customer mix. As marketing strategies are developed to target specific types of customer, or customer groups, understanding the relative profitability enables the investment appraisal of future marketing spend.

Cost of Acquisition

CPA can highlight the cost of obtaining new customers and the benefit of retaining existing customers as retention rates and acquisition costs can be taken into account to establish the benefit from various marketing strategies. This knowledge is built up over a period of time by close monitoring of the marketing strategy and its impact.

Product and Market Development for Profitable Customers

CPA highlights whether strategies such as product development or market development are appropriate, for example, new products to profitable customers, or seeking more profitable market channels or segments.

Costs to Serve

The basic principle behind customer profitability analysis is that costs can be allocated to individual customers, or customer groupings. These are known as the costs to serve. Most accounting systems are set up to measure product profitability and reflect administrative groupings, such as cost centers, rather than customer groupings. Therefore undertaking CPA on a regular basis to monitor changes and make strategic decisions may require a change to the accounting systems in order to be able to provide a meaningful analysis.

Ideally CPA should be carried out by directly allocating costs to customers or customer groups. However, some costs such as administration costs in raising invoices and so on can be allocated to customers, but the acid test is really whether or not supplying the customer saves the cost. In other words, the question that determines whether the cost is allocated to customers or not is: If the organization stops supplying the customer is the cost still incurred? If the answer is yes, then the cost should not be allocated to the customer. Apportioning costs across customers detracts from the analysis. Only those costs that directly relate to the customer or customer group should be allocated.

These costs can differ between customers due to factors such as order size, frequency, complexity, distance from warehouse, and negotiating power in the hands of the customer linked to strategic importance, as well as method of purchase such as online or instore. The technique of ABC (see Chapter 5) can be utilized to enhance the allocation of costs to customers and customer groups based on the level of activity generated by the type of customer.

The types of costs that arise from customer activity are illustrated in Table 3.1 within the typical CPA report.

Table 3.1 Customer profitability analysis report

		$	
Sales revenue from actual product mix		267,000	100%
Less sales discounts		(1,000)	
Net invoice amount		266,000	
Less sales returns and allowances		(2,000)	
Net sales revenue		264,000	
Less direct product costs		(132,000)	

(Continued)

Table 3.1 (*Continued*)

Product contribution		132,000	49.4%
Less customer costs:			
Order processing and cost of invoicing	(1,500)		
Sales visits	(5,000)		
Cost of dealing with returns	(500)		
Distribution costs	(15,000)		
Cost of customer-specific promotions	(6,000)		
Costs of holding customer-specific inventory	(2,000)		
Cost of financing of outstanding receivables	(5,000)		
Costs to serve	(35,000)	(35,000)	
Customer contribution		97,000	36.3%

Such a report can highlight the difference between the costs of servicing different individuals or companies, which can be utilized to identify those customers that are expensive to serve and thus look for ways of reducing customer-specific costs, or indeed transferring the cost to the customer. The financial consequences of losing a customer can also be ascertained as well as identifying ways of making the unprofitable customers more profitable, or indeed of making profitable customers more profitable. The direct costs of goods or services should also be considered as the mix of products that a customer purchases can impact on the overall contribution that the customer makes to the fixed costs and profit of the organization.

It is important to realize that this is not a precise science. Subjective decisions are inevitable. Customer profitability analysis is just a part of the wider customer analysis and other factors should be taken into account, such as strategic importance of the customer, discussed earlier. The important point is that organizations gain a better understanding of the business and the customer base from having undertaken the analysis. Ideally organizations should be providing profitable products to profitable customers, so simply undertaking customer profitability analysis does not mean that the direct product profitability analysis is ignored. Every product does not necessarily carry the same margin, due to operational costs or functionality. The trick to a successful strategy is not just attracting customers, but encouraging them, via marketing and promotions to purchase higher margin products. This illustrates the link between product profitability, customer profitability, operational decisions, and marketing strategies.

Forms of Customer Profitability and Relationship to the Customer

Lind and Stromsten (2006) identified different forms of customer profitability analysis and the circumstances under which each might be appropriate: individual customer profitability analysis, customer segment profitability analysis, lifetime customer profitability analysis, and valuation of customers as an asset. The difference between the individual *customer profitability* and *customer segment profitability* analysis is related to the idea of the analysis being appropriate for individual or groups of customers respectively. As discussed earlier, business-to-business organizations may be able to undertake individual customer analysis, but an organization serving consumer markets may be able to identify segments or types, such as online versus in-store, or demographic/geographic groupings or sociocultural groupings.

Customer profitability analysis is often based on historical information, but to gauge a customer's true worth to the organization it is necessary to consider not just past performance but future performance as well. This leads to assessing profitability over the lifetime of the customer and is the basis of *lifetime customer profitability*. This technique recognizes that as the relationship grows the customer has potential to become more profitable in future years, thus yielding significant profits and benefits to the organization over its lifetime. It is recognized that while some customers may be unprofitable in the short term they have potential to grow and become very valuable in the future, such as new and growing organizations. The concept of *customers as assets* or *economic value of the customer* attempts to value the customer in terms of the net present value of the future revenue streams minus the costs. This is dealt with in the marketing literature as *customer lifetime value* or CLV.

A common formula applied to calculate the CLV is:

$$CLV = \sum_{t=1}^{t=n} \frac{(M_t - C_t) \times (\text{retention rate}_t)^{t-1}}{(1+i)^t} - \text{Initial acquisition cost}$$

M_t = the margin (revenue less marginal product cost) from customer in year t

C_t = any additional costs to serve (and retain) the customer in year t

i = cost of capital (often the weighted average cost of capital)

The calculation assumes several factors can be ascertained or estimated such as the probability of retaining customers over a period of time and the cost of retaining them, for example, customer-sustaining costs and the profit margin earned by each customer including the costs to serve. The discounted cash flows earned from the lifetime of the customer are compared to the acquisition costs. This is an area where accountants and marketing professionals working together can provide valuable insight into understanding the optimum customer portfolio for the organization to target. By analyzing the costs and activities over a period of time experience can be built up to make the model more accurate. This is particularly useful for banks where gaining a customer as a student and retaining them through employment to retirement provides the opportunity to sell many products and services. Based on this information it is possible to determine the level of marketing investment that could be afforded on the acquisition of new customers to ensure that an adequate return on investment was earned.

Customer Portfolio Management

Customer profitability and key attributes of customers can be used to review a portfolio of customers. Portfolio analysis can be undertaken using a range of factors for axes such as volume purchased and frequency of purchase. Utilizing customer profitability as one of the axes can prove to be highly informative, especially when set alongside a measure that relates to customer potential.

A customer rating can be ascertained for each customer based on a range of factors, which could include:

- Loyalty—reference to past purchases and number of other suppliers with which the customer does business.
- Core market—the industry sector it is in, that is, is it in a core market serviced by the organization?
- Finance—reference to payment record and financial strength.
- Value-added factor—is there potential for the organization to add value to the customer?
- Growth potential—the potential of the customer to grow and generate future sales.
- Degree of support required—how demanding they are as a customer? Are they a high-maintenance customer?

These factors are given a score of between 1 and 5 and then combined to create an overall weighted rating of between 1 and 5 for the customer. Weightings can be applied to factors as determined by the organization. The position is then plotted on a grid with the axes denoting profitability and rating as illustrated in Figure 3.4.

The rating produced has an element of subjectivity but the grid provides a basis for discussions, such as how the position of customer B could be improved. Or whether customer B has the potential and is worth investing resources in order to nurture the customer to achieve

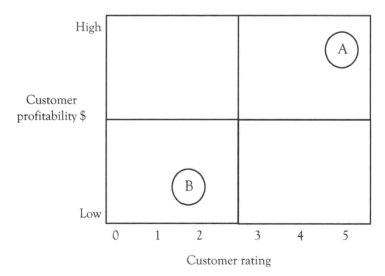

Figure 3.4 Customer-positioning grid

a higher position on the grid. Ideally the organization needs to target other customers with similar characteristics to customer A. The analysis can indicate profitable segments within a market to which customer A belongs. This can also be utilized as a motivational tool for sales personnel to improve the customer profitability associated with individual sales staff who take responsibility for specific customers, such as key accounts.

Value Creation System

Customers are prepared to pay more for the goods and services than it costs to produce or provide them, due to the value they perceive is added by the organization. Customers are essentially paying for the value added. Organizations choose to undertake certain activities in order to add value to the customer. Porter (1985) suggests that competitive advantage arises out of the way in which organizations manage and perform activities. Thinking about the organization as a value creation system offers a model of corporate activities that can be utilized to analyze what an organization does and hence improve where it can add value to the customer. It helps to ascertain how value is created, how costs are caused, and how competitive advantage can be gained. A key factor in its application is that the objective is to add value to the customer and hence helps to develop a customer focus to the organization's activities.

A basic value system is illustrated in Figure 3.5.

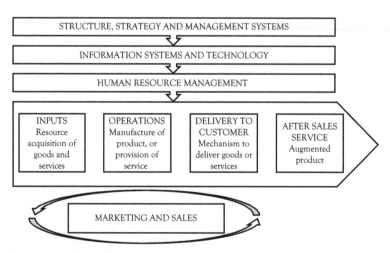

Figure 3.5 The value creation system

The inputs and resource acquisition involve the activities of receiving, handling, and storing of inputs required to undertake the operations of the organization.

Operations involves the activities of converting inputs into outputs such as manufacturing a motor vehicle. The operations in the service sector are represented by the activities involved in providing the service, for example, in the provision of the meal in the restaurant, the provision of a haircut, carrying out an audit, or providing consultancy advice.

The delivery to the customer mechanism involves storing the product prior to purchase if appropriate and its distribution to customers. This is essentially getting the product or service to the customer. Therefore in the case of a venue, such as a theater, night club, or university, the location is a key element of the delivery mechanism. In the case of an entertainment venue a key factor in its success is whether the customer can get to and from the venue easily? Therefore, transport links are an important consideration in the delivery mechanism.

Marketing and sales involves informing the customers about the product or service, persuading them to buy it and facilitating their ability to do so. This will include decisions concerning marketing strategy and means of selling, such as whether to utilize a physical sales force or online systems. In cases where products are manufactured to customer order marketing and sales impacts on the acquisition of resources as much as the final product. This therefore spans the activities of inputs from suppliers, operations, and delivery. Indeed in a customer-focused business the marketing and sales activity determines the level of production required.

After-sales service includes activities such as installing products, repairing, upgrading, and so forth including customer care programs. Basically anything that is provided after the customer has received the main product or enjoyed the service. In marketing terms this is sometimes referred to as augmenting the product and therefore there is often a fine line between the product produced from operations and the after-sales service, that is, when does the operations element stop?

Functions such as human resource management, IT systems, and the organization's structure, strategy and management systems support the primary activities. These activities support all of the activities undertaken to provide the product or service to the customer.

The way an organization chooses to configure its activities can provide the means for competitive advantage. An organization can choose which activities it needs to undertake to satisfy customer needs. For example, organizations may opt not to provide any after-sales service.

Part of the design of the value system is in managing the interlinkages and ensuring that all activities undertaken add value. It is of no benefit if the organization has the capacity to manufacture products to customer order within a short time frame if suppliers are not able to provide the same flexibility. The way around this might be to hold high levels of inventory, but this incurs unnecessary cost, which could be reduced by better management of the inputs and management of the supply chain, perhaps via use of technology and just-in-time systems.

There is also an information flow around the value creation system and this needs to be facilitated. If the organization's competitive advantage is to manufacture to customer demand the information flow from the customer, via the marketing and sales activities, backward through the value system, even to the extent of procuring component parts from suppliers, needs to be highly efficient. This requires an effective management system potentially supported by technology. Therefore, the competitive advantage is in the efficient operation of the value creation system as a whole.

Utilizing Value Creation System Analysis

The analysis of the value creation system can be used to identify potential activities that could be outsourced. It, therefore, sets up strategic debates within the organization. It could be said that if an activity is not critical then it could become a candidate for outsourcing. This is also said of nonvalue-adding activities.

There is a trend toward outsourcing the basic accounting functions to specialist firms as they are seen as nonvalue adding but essential activities. In other words, the focus is on performing the activities as efficiently and cost effectively as possible. However, consider an organization such as Flying Flowers. This is an organization that began delivering fresh flowers to customers within a region known as the Channel Islands off the coast of the United Kingdom and covered a relatively narrow geographical area. As the organization expanded its global reach the requirement of key logistical capabilities in order to deliver fresh flowers became more strategic as it formed the basis of the competitive advantage, that is, fresh flowers for next-day delivery. As the expertise of the organization lies in growing flowers outsourcing the logistical activity to a specialist logistics organization made strategic sense and was more cost-effective.

Each organization configures the value creation system to suit its own needs. The competitive advantage may come from how the value system is configured, which activities the organization chooses to do itself, and which it chooses to allow others to do, even the customers.

Consider the case of Dell (Figure 3.6), an organization that sells computers online with the marketing proposition of tailoring products to meet the specific requirements of customers, and IKEA (Figure 3.7), an organization that predominantly sells flat-pack home furnishings from out-of-town stores. IKEA has stores around the world, three of which are in the United States.

The principle behind Dell is to add a significant amount of value to the customer, while keeping costs low, whereas IKEA encourages the customers to do as much as possible for themselves, in order to keep costs and prices low. In the early days of IKEA the customer did nearly all of

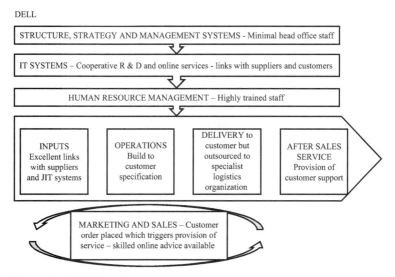

Figure 3.6 DELL value system

IKEA

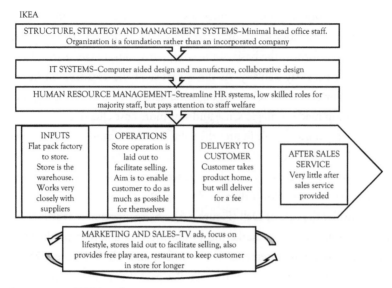

Figure 3.7 IKEA value system

the work including selecting products for themselves, taking the product home, and assembling the product. Over the years IKEA has responded competitively by offering these services but as an optional extra for additional cost. This retains their core market offering to customers who want a value for money product but also enables them to attract customers who are prepared to pay extra for the additional added value.

As every organization has a value system of its own, managing the supply chain involves managing an extended value system in that each organization is adding value to the customer. The way an organization adds value through the extended value system is an important aspect of creating competitive advantage, so supply chain management and customer relationship management become more important to today's organization.

As the value creation system is concerned with activities, ABC can be utilized as part of the analysis. The activities become the cost drivers and are the result of strategic choices made by the management of an organization, which determines its underlying cost base. It can therefore be utilized to support the development and maintenance of the competitive strategy of cost leadership or differentiation, that is, all activities undertaken should support, and be consistent with, the overall competitive strategy of the organization. However, activities do not manage themselves and therefore it requires activity-based management (ABM) to reap the full benefits (see Chapter 5).

Supplier Analysis

The benefit of utilizing the concept of a value creation system is that it is customer-focused, that is, focuses on adding value to the customer. However, as discussed earlier the value creation system embraces the supply chain and therefore it is worth taking a few moments to understand the significance of suppliers.

The Three Elements Related to Supplier Analysis

Supplier Appraisal

Supplier appraisal is an assessment of a potential supplier's capability of meeting and maintaining the key elements contained within the contract, such as quality standards, delivery commitments, quantity, and price.

Supplier Approval

Once the supplier has been assessed and found to be capable of meeting the contract requirements the suppler is placed on an approved supplier list.

Supplier Rating

The performance of the supplier is monitored against the terms of the contract. An index can be created that ranks suppliers in terms of performance to determine the preferred supplier list. Large organizations often maintain an approved supplier list to which suppliers may be seeking access. In terms of supplier/buyer power relationships it is worth remembering that an organization is a supplier's customer and they may well have undertaken customer profitability analysis to determine the status of the organization as a customer. Therefore there is a concept of making an organization attractive to suppliers in order to obtain a good working relationship. The mutual benefit can be a determining factor in the success of a long-term profitable relationship for both parties.

As with customers it is possible to rate the supplier performance and ascertain the strategic importance of the relationship. Typical factors of performance that can be monitored include the normal aspects such as delivery performance and price, but also the ability of the supplier to respond to changes in demand. Referring back to the value creation system, if an organization's competitive advantage is based on its ability to respond to customer demand, the same degree of responsiveness and flexibility needs to be present in the supply chain. One way to deal with this might be to dual source with the suppliers' full knowledge of why the organization chooses to do so. This can be the basis of deciding the strategic importance of various suppliers and the development of supplier relationships conducive to both parties. The balance of negotiating power becomes relevant in the discussion about price and contract terms. Developing strong supplier relationships can mitigate against supplier power as discussed under industry analysis in Chapter 2. Other aspects of supplier analysis can include an estimate of the likely costs of a breakdown in the supply chain. World events such as natural disasters can affect an organization that relies on global supplies by disrupting the supply chain. The number of suppliers that can provide a product or service, the degree of competition in the demand/supply market, for example, for scarce resources, and substitution possibilities all impact on the supplier relationship and accountants can aid the evaluation of the strategic/financial risk these factors pose. More obvious aspects such as make or buy decisions, which could be the basis of a competitive advantage, provide opportunities for accountants to contribute. Supplier evaluation, however, is situational and there may be instances where it is imperative, such as in the negotiation of a service level agreement. The aspects that the evaluation focuses on will relate to the requirements of the particular relationship, but all evaluations will probably include aspects such as finance, production capacity and facilities, information technology, human resources, quality, performance, and environmental and ethical considerations.

Financial Analysis

One of the key areas in which the accountant is able to provide a substantial contribution to the internal analysis is in the assessment of the current and projected financial position and performance. This can be a source of both a strength and weakness and can have a significant influence on what strategies are adopted in the future and also on the organizational ability to deliver or undertake the strategies in terms of financing the strategic initiatives. It is important to undertake a full analysis of the performance of the organization as a whole and of any business units that exist within the organization. This analysis can also be undertaken on the major competitors as part of competitor analysis, where financial information is available to identify their financial strengths and weaknesses.

The basis of this analysis can be accomplished via financial ratio analysis. However, more detailed analysis of product costs, product contribution, and customer profitability analysis should also be undertaken. The more detailed analysis is difficult for competitor analysis, but financial ratio analysis of competitors from the annual report and accounts is nearly always possible, certainly for competitors that are registered corporate entities. The analysis is not just a static analysis, that is, a review of one year, but an analysis over time to identify trends in performance and projections into the future. An organization's strategic plan will inevitably be expressed in financial terms and therefore establishing the likelihood of achieving the financial objectives, given the current strategy and evaluating the impact of changes to strategy, is key to the strategic management process.

The ratios that are discussed in this section do not represent the totality of ratios that can be calculated, but indicate typical high-level ratios that can be used to assess the financial performance of an organization or strategic business unit.

Gross Profit Percentage

$$\frac{\text{Gross profit}}{\text{Sales revenue}} \times 100 = x\%$$

Gross profit is the difference between the sales value and the cost of goods sold. In a manufacturing environment the cost of goods sold would include the cost of manufacturing, the detailed elements of which would be monitored closely via cost control measures. In an organization that purchases products for onward sale this can be utilized as a measure of purchasing effectiveness and can indicate the potential emergence of supplier power or buyer power in the industry. For example, if costs are rising and the organization is unable to pass on cost increases to customers the margin will reduce. Similarly if there is downward pressure on prices from customers, and increasing levels of competition on price, the margin will reduce. Ideally the organization is seeking to at least maintain the margin from year to year. Reductions in margins can be an early warning sign of problems to come later.

Operating Profit Percentage

$$\frac{\text{Operating profit}}{\text{Sales revenue}} \times 100 = x\%$$

By deducting the operating costs from the gross margin the operating profit is obtained. Further analysis can be undertaken to ascertain trends within the operating costs that require attention. A reduction in operating profit could result from a gross margin reduction but can also indicate that the operating costs need careful investigation. The operating profit is also taken before interest and tax. This is significant when using this ratio for competitor analysis as this makes the comparison more meaningful. Interest payments are affected by the way an organization has chosen to finance itself and therefore this could affect profit levels taken after interest payments, and tax reflects the tax regimes where the organization does business. However, it is a valid assumption that organizations in the same sector face similar operating costs and therefore a difference in operating profit could be due to different operational decisions and efficiencies.

Return on Capital Employed (ROCE)

$$\frac{\text{Operating profit}}{\text{Capital employed}} \times 100 = x\%$$

The return on capital employed provides a means of measuring how effectively the organization is utilizing the capital employed within the business. Capital employed can be analyzed into share capital and loan capital. The mix of this is known as the capital structure and can be monitored via the gearing ratio. The definition of capital employed can be slightly different in that some definitions will include total equity (shareholders' funds) and all of the noncurrent liabilities, whereas other definitions will include total equity and only long-term borrowings. So long as the ratio is calculated on a consistent basis a valid comparison between years and with competitors can be made. This is true of any ratio—the inclusion of items on a consistent basis provides a valid comparison.

Asset Turnover

$$\frac{\text{Sales revenue}}{\text{Capital employed}} = \text{number of times}$$

The asset turnover is another ratio where various formats can be utilized. It is also possible to use the total assets, or net assets, or noncurrent assets to produce a ratio. The ratio shown here utilizes the capital employed as this creates a relationship between the operating profit and the return on capital employed. This provides a means of monitoring how well the organization is utilizing the capital within the business.

The asset turnover as shown indicates the revenue that is generated from every dollar of capital invested. The higher this figure becomes the more effective the organization is at generated revenue from the capital invested. This can be used in divisional performance management to set targets for both operating profit and asset turnover. An increase in either will result in an increase in return on capital employed. This is illustrated as follows.

$$\frac{\text{Operating profit}}{\text{Sales revenue}} \times \frac{\text{Sales revenue}}{\text{Capital employed}} = \frac{\text{Operating profit}}{\text{Capital employed}}$$

It can be seen that the sales revenues in the equation will cancel each other out to leave the formula for return on capital employed.

Gearing Ratio

$$\frac{\text{Long-term Borrowings}}{\text{Equity} + \text{Long-term Borrowings}} \times 100 = x\%$$

The gearing ratio indicates the proportion of total capital that is represented by borrowings. The significance is that loans require interest payments, which are contractual, so must be paid whether the organization makes a profit or not. High levels of gearing become problematic when economic conditions make trading difficult thus putting downward pressure on the gross profit and operating profit. The interest, however, must still be paid, which could put the organization into financial difficulties. The mix of capital will have an impact on how easy it is for an organization to raise funds to finance new strategic initiatives. It also has an impact on the cost of capital, which is often used as a discount factor in investment appraisals (see Chapter 7) and therefore the management accountant has an interest in the capital structure of the organization.

Return on Shareholders' Funds or Equity

$$\frac{\text{Profit after interest and tax}}{\text{Total equity (also known as shareholders' funds)}} \times 100 = x\%$$

The return on shareholders' funds provides an indicator of performance from the shareholder perspective. The profit here is after interest and tax so that the profit is what is left for shareholders. Like the gearing ratio this can also have an impact on an organization's ability to raise finance for future strategies.

Working Capital Management

An organization requires a certain amount of capital to manage the operations. For example, staff and suppliers may need to be paid before the organization receives money from the customers, especially if credit periods apply. This is called working capital and a series of ratios can be utilized to monitor this aspect of the business.

Working Capital Ratio—Current Ratio

$$\frac{\text{Current assets}}{\text{Current liabilities}} = \text{number of times}$$

An organization needs to know that it can pay its current liabilities when required. As a general rule in order to have some comfort this ratio needs to indicate that current assets exceed current liabilities, but it is dependent on the industry sector. For example, in some businesses where customers normally pay in cash or via credit card such as retailing, organizations are able to survive quite happily on a ratio of less than 1:1.

Quick Ratio

$$\frac{\text{Current assets - inventory}}{\text{Current liabilities}} = \text{number of times}$$

As it takes time to convert inventory into cash, if it is sold on credit, the quick ratio tests whether an organization can fulfill its current liability obligations at short notice from more liquid sources. The receivables element of current assets can be turned into cash quite quickly by utilizing the services of a collection agency that provides the cash to the organization (usually less a fee) and then recoups the cash from the organization's customers. The impact this may have on customer relationships needs to be considered if an organization chooses this as a collection strategy, as customers may resent being approached by a third party. This highlights the need to consider the wider implications of decisions and not to take decisions based on numerical analysis only.

Receivables Days

$$\frac{\text{Trade receivables}}{\text{Sales revenue from credit sales}} \times 365 = \text{number of days}$$

The receivables days measures how long it takes customers to pay. It is more appropriate to use credit sales as the divider to this equation as these are the sales that generate the receivables on the balance sheet. When calculating the ratio for competitors from published accounts, however, it is often not possible to distinguish the credit sales from cash sales. This is where experience can help as if an organization typically makes very few cash sales then it is a fair assumption that competitors have the same split of cash and credit sales.

Payables Days

$$\frac{\text{Trade payables}}{\text{Purchases}} \times 365 = \text{number of days}$$

The payables days measures how long it takes the organization to pay its suppliers. Trade payables should always be paid within the agreed credit terms, but this does not always happen. Ideally organizations do not want to pay their suppliers faster than they receive the cash from their own customers so their balance of the receivable and payables days is significant for cash flow. As with the receivable days, when calculating the ratio for competitors the purchases figure is not always available and therefore the use of cost of goods sold can be used as a substitute for purchases.

Inventory Days

$$\frac{\left(\text{Opening} + \text{Closing Inventory}\right)/2\right)}{\text{Cost of goods sold}} \times 365 = \text{number of days goods held in inventory}$$

The inventory days measures the average time that the organization holds goods in inventory prior to the sale. In inventory management this would be calculated for most product lines or groups to identify the presence of slow-moving items. However, the overall number of days is useful as a measure from year to year to ensure that the amount of capital tied up in inventory is not excessive. When calculating the ratio for competitors it may be necessary to use the closing inventory figure rather than calculating the average inventory.

Interest Cover

$$\frac{\text{Profit before interest and tax}}{\text{Interest charges}} = \text{number of times}$$

The interest cover indicates how easily the organization can meet its obligations to debt providers and pay the interest when due. This links closely to the level of gearing as high gearing can mean high interest charges and could put the organization in financial difficulties if, during the environmental analysis, it is noticed that interest rates may be increased in the future.

Earnings Per Share

$$\frac{\text{Profit for the year (after interest and tax)}}{\text{Number of shares in issue}} = \text{Value of earnings per share}$$

The earnings per share (EPS) is an investment indictor and can determine how easily an organization can attract additional funds from equity markets. The higher the EPS the more attractive the organization's share may be.

An Example of Ratio Analysis

Suppose that both X Inc. and Y Inc. sell electrical goods to retailers, that is, they are in the same industry sector, but are based in different geographical areas of the same country. The income statements and balance sheets for one year are shown in appendix B and the resultant ratios are shown in Table 3.2.

Table 3.2 Financial ratios for X Inc. and Y Inc.

	X Inc.	Y Inc.
Gross profit percentage	25.0	20.0
Operating profit percentage	12.75	13.3
Return on capital employed	26.15%	11.6%
Return on equity	19.5%	10.7%
Asset turnover	2.05	0.87
Current ratio	1.1	1.9
Quick ratio/acid test	0.79	1.09
Gearing	N/A	58%
Interest cover	N/A	2
Inventory days	48.7	61
Receivables days	73	55
Payables days	91	61

The best approach would be to analyze the performance over a period of time, but for the purposes of illustration we could make the following observations based on the financial statements for one year.

X Inc. has a higher gross profit percentage than Y Inc. This could be due to differences in the pricing strategy as well as sales mix. It might also be due to the supplier relationship that X or Y has developed and their ability to negotiate costs with suppliers. For example, if X was able to purchase goods at lower prices the company would be able to keep costs lower and increase its margin. Another explanation may be that as the companies operate in different parts of the country the economic conditions in the different parts of the country may impact on the prices that can be charged.

The operating profit percentage is about the same level for both companies. This indicates that X has higher operating costs, for example, distribution, selling, and administration costs, than Y. Following through the fact that they operate in different parts of the country this may also contribute to the difference in operating costs, for example, establishment costs such as rent, distribution costs, salary levels, and so on. However, this would need investigating further.

X achieves a higher ROCE than Y, which is due to the better asset utilization (asset turnover). This means that X utilizes the capital employed much more effectively than Y. This is also followed through into the return on equity where X achieves a better return for the shareholders.

In relation to liquidity Y has a higher current ratio than X and therefore is slightly more liquid, which means it is in a better position to pay its current liabilities as they fall due. However X should not be worried as its current ratio is 1.1 and therefore is in a position to pay its liabilities. However when looking at the quick ratio X falls below 1 whereas Y is at 1.09:1, leaving Y in a better position.

Y however has gearing of 58 percent, which is relatively high creating a high interest charge, but it is able to cover this twice so is managing to pay its interest from profit. X on the other hand has no gearing, using long-term finance entirely from equity sources.

Y has inventory days of 61 and X of 48.7. It would be useful to identify what level of inventory is normal for this business, but both companies could probably benefit from reducing this level, and releasing the cash tied up in inventory. In terms of receivable days and payable days X has 73 and 91 days, respectively, whereas Y has 55 and 61 days, respectively. Both companies could benefit from managing their receivables and payables at lower levels. X, with creditor days of 91, is probably becoming unethical in its treatment of suppliers unless it has negotiated longer credit terms as part of the supplier agreement.

Management Accounting in Support of Internal Appraisal

9Ms

Assisting in the evaluation of the 9M's elements and the financial impact of addressing any shortfalls (e.g., replacing plant and machinery, costs of recruitment and training of employees, arranging suitable finance, and evaluating the profitability of new products and markets).

Portfolio Analysis

Evaluating strategies emanating from the portfolio analysis such as financing investment requirements, monitoring the profitability and cash generation properties of product combinations, and changes in the balance of the product portfolio.

Product Life Cycle

Ensuring that appropriate accounting techniques are utilized at each stage of the product life cycle and portfolio classification of products. Assisting in the development of new products via target costing and life cycle costing techniques and pricing (discussed in Chapter 6).

Customer Profitability Analysis

Undertaking customer profitability analysis and working closely with marketing personnel to develop strategies to promote the acquisition and retention of profitable customers. Ascertaining and monitoring the costs and assisting in the development of strategies to enhance customer profitability across the whole portfolio of customers.

ABC and Value System

Utilizing ABC techniques to aid the analysis of the value system to ascertain where value can be enhanced and support strategies of cost leadership and differentiation (see Chapter 5) throughout the value system.

Supplier Analysis

Assisting in the evaluation and monitoring of suppliers to ensure consistency with the overall competitive strategy of cost leadership or differentiation and working, where necessary, to reduce the incidence of supplier power (e.g., assisting in negotiations with suppliers).

Financial Evaluation

Evaluating the financial strengths and weaknesses of the company and developing a financial strategy to ensure that the right amount of finance is available, at the right time and for the right cost.

CHAPTER 4

Corporate Appraisal

The Corporate Appraisal SWOT Analysis

The corporate appraisal is also known as the SWOT analysis—strengths, weaknesses, opportunities, and threats. Primarily strengths and weaknesses come from the internal appraisal and opportunities and threats come from the environmental analysis.

Changes in the business environment are identified during the environmental analysis phase, but it is only when these are matched against the organization's ability to deal with the change that it becomes evident whether the change represents an opportunity or a threat.

For example, proposed changes to the regulatory environment could present opportunities for expansion and product/market development if the organization has the resources. However, if the organization has few resources, such that dealing with the changes will be problematic, it could pose a threat to its ability to meet the strategic objectives. This is significant for competitor analysis as understanding the potential impact of changes in the environment on competitors compared to the organization is a key part of developing a sustainable competitive strategy.

The cruciform diagram shown in Figure 4.1 is often used to construct a SWOT. This ideally limits the number of elements that are eventually included. In reality there will be many elements that could be included, some of which are subjective. The key is that the SWOT elements are prioritized and reduced to a manageable number.

The axes denote that strengths and weaknesses are relative to the competition. This is significant in determining what the actual strength or weakness might be. For example, if an organization considers that it has a very experienced and highly skilled workforce, it may classify this as a strength. But if the competitor organizations in the industry also have a very experienced and highly skilled workforce, then this may not be

Internal: Relative to competitor organizations

STRENGTHS Build / Match with opportunities	WEAKNESSES Address / Remedy / Convert to strength
OPPORTUNITIES Grasp / take advantage	THREATS Avoid / Minimize / Convert to opportunities

External: Present for all industry members

Figure 4.1 Typical cruciform chart layout for SWOT

the true source of the strength and hence a competitive advantage. The organization that manages its workforce more effectively may be able to achieve a competitive advantage indicating that its real strength is the ability to manage the workforce more effectively than the competition, not the highly skilled workforce itself. This illustrates that SWOT can be quite subjective. It is sometimes difficult to assess the aspect of "relative to the competition" as it is difficult to gain enough accurate information about the competitors to be able to make an objective judgment. Therefore, in reality the strengths and weaknesses are not always assessed against the competition.

The opportunities and threats originate in the environment and thus are available to all industry members. As with the strengths and weaknesses, there is a degree of subjectivity and discretion in the practical determination of opportunities and threats. There is a subtle difference between what might be described as a strategic option available to one organization and an opportunity that is present for all industry members. For practical purposes an opportunity is something that presents itself from the environmental analysis as being a possible strategic option that the organization can pursue. Another area of subjectivity that arises is deciding whether changes in the environment present a threat or represent a weakness. The best way to decide between the two is to determine whether the organization has direct control over the outcome. If it does, then it is probably internal and represents a weakness as the organization can address the issue directly. If, however, the source is external the organization may be able to influence, but not directly control, the event. In this case it is best viewed as a threat for which there is still some uncertainty about the outcome and hence the organization needs to formulate, and be prepared to implement, an appropriate response.

The intension is to match strengths to opportunities. If weaknesses are addressed so that they no longer represent a weakness, what was once a threat, due to the organization's inability to deal with it, may become an opportunity. Based on the SWOT analysis a good strategy will build on the strengths, address the weaknesses, grasp the opportunities, and avoid or minimize the threats.

The use of the cruciform chart helps in the prioritization of the strengths, weaknesses, and so on, so that it provides a focus for competitive advantage and management attention. The technique of strategic factor analysis can be utilized to aid the development and evaluation of strategic options. In this technique the elements of the SWOT are prioritized, ranked, and given a weighting. For example, consider the analysis of strengths in Table 4.1.

The same process would be done for weaknesses, opportunities, and threats. Then for each strategic option the various combinations of elements of the SWOT can be evaluated to provide an overall score. So the overall assessment of the strategic option A may be represented in Table 4.2.

Table 4.1 Factor analysis and weighting of strengths

Factor— Strengths	Weighting	Ranking	Weighted ranking score
Strong brand identity	20%	3	0.6
Strategic locations	10%	4	0.4
Innovative product range	30%	1	0.3
Highly skilled workforce	40%	2	0.8
Total			2.1

Table 4.2 Factor analysis score for strategy A

Factor	Weighting	Ranking	Weighted ranking score
Key strength 1	30%	1	0.3
Key strength 2	40%	2	0.8
Key weakness 1	40%	1	0.4
Key opportunity 2	30%	2	0.6
Key threat 1	50%	1	0.5
Total strategy A			2.6

The various strategies could be compared and utilized as part of the decision-making process. However, a problem with this approach is that strategy cannot be reduced to a set of numbers and therefore, although providing some information on likely outcomes, it should never be the sole basis for deciding the future strategy. It also carries with it a high degree of subjective judgment despite being represented by a numerical analysis.

GAP Analysis

GAP analysis is concerned with identifying whether there is a gap between what the organization wants to achieve and the likely outcome if it continues with the existing strategy. It can be illustrated by Figure 4.2.

The starting point is the current situation, that is, now. The objective is plotted over a period of time. This is usually expressed in years with a time frame of three to five years or possibly longer, but obviously the level of accuracy reduces the further ahead the forecast extends into the future. The objective can be anything that qualifies as an objective and that can be quantified. It is more often than not a profit objective, or sales growth, but could equally be that the organization needs to increase the number of skilled employees over a five-year period. For example, in the health care industry or hospitals, there may be targets to recruit and train a specific number of new nurses and health professionals over the next five years. The objective is therefore the number of new health care

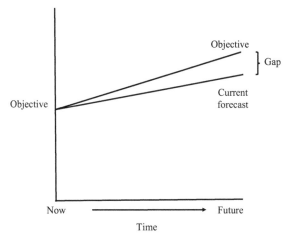

Figure 4.2 GAP analysis

professionals to be recruited. The strategy is the recruitment and retention strategy and concerned with the pay and benefits package.

The next step is to look at the current strategy and to forecast or extrapolate what will happen if the organization continues on that path. In the instance of a profit objective this is easy to envisage, but for the recruitment of nurses the forecast would relate to how many additional nurses would be recruited if the organization follows the existing recruitment strategy with the same pay and benefits package. Invariably the result is that there is a gap between the objective and projected outcome. The accountant can provide valuable advice in determining how big the gap is, particularly when assessed as a profits gap, and the potential impact if the gap is not addressed.

The next phase is to evaluate the various strategic options to see how far they go to closing the gap. Gaps can arise due to internal or external factors, which is why the strategic management process is iterative and a continuous or periodic process, not a one-off exercise. For example, suppose that the strategic option chosen to close the gap is to launch a new product or enter a new market. Competitors will respond and therefore, although there is a short-term closing of the gap, it begins to open up again due to competitor response. It is therefore advisable to undertake continuous gap analysis, whereby the analysis is undertaken on a frequent basis, such as once every quarter or six months.

Another possibility is to take a realistic view and reassess the objectives. It is not cheating or moving the goal posts, but realistically assessing the objectives given the changes in the business environment. For example, when the financial crisis occurred in 2008 many organizations were suddenly in survival mode rather than moving forward on a growth trajectory, as may have been originally planned. Often political changes in many countries impact on an organization's ability to achieve current objectives and change their view of the future, perhaps putting growth plans and investment decisions on hold until the outcome becomes clearer. Thus, organizations may be reassessing the strategic objectives for the next few years, and setting more realistic or amended targets.

Management Accounting in Support of Corporate Appraisal

Strengths and Weaknesses

The accountant is able to assist in the evaluation of strengths and weaknesses, particularly in terms of financial strengths and weaknesses. This could be via the financial analysis undertaken as part of the internal analysis.

Financial Impact

Identifying the potential financial impact of environmental changes helps to determine whether changes represent an opportunity or a threat.

Size of Gap

Identifying the size of any gap that exists between the objectives and forecast outturn in financial terms, given the current strategy.

Evaluation of Options

Evaluating the potential options based on combinations of strengths and weaknesses can help determine the most successful options to close the gap. This can include strategies such as implementing a cost reduction exercise.

CHAPTER 5

Competitive Strategies

The Generic Competitive Strategies

There are essentially three elements for a successful competitive strategy: unique, sustainable, and relevant. Unique means that nobody else is doing it, and coupled with sustainability means that it is not easily replicated. This is the difficult element in a competitive market. Relevant means that it is relevant to the customer, which maintains the customer focus required for success in today's business environment.

Porter (1980) identified the generic strategies for competitive advantage. These strategies help to determine the basis of competition, whether cost-driven or value-driven (differentiation), and the competitive scope. It is about positioning the organization in the market, that is, it is a conscious choice.

Cost Leadership

A cost leadership strategy seeks to achieve the position of lowest cost producer in the industry. By achieving the lowest production cost, a manufacturer can compete on price with every other producer in the market, and earn the higher unit profits. There are several strategies that aid cost leadership.

Economies of Scale

Economies of scale requires high volumes of production and possibly a limited variation in the product offering, that is, standardization of products. Mature markets may become fragmented, as the focus moves toward products targeted at specific segments of the market, which can undermine the advantage as the cost base rises and some of the economies of scale can be lost.

Technological Advantage

The use of technology can help reduce costs and enhance productivity. Techniques include computer-aided design, computer-aided manufacturing, just-in-time purchasing, inventory management systems, and flexible manufacturing systems.

Exploiting the Effects of the Learning Curve

Organizations become more efficient over time and, as the expertise increases, this can result in lower average unit costs. This makes it more difficult for new entrants who have less expertise in the production process to obtain the same degree of efficiency. This can create a barrier to entry and reduce the threat of new entrants to the industry. New technologies, however, can undermine this advantage creating a threat of new entrants, illustrating the need to monitor the environment.

Lean Thinking

Adopting the principles of lean thinking can also help to support a strategy of cost leadership. This involves constantly looking to eliminate inefficiencies in the systems and minimizing overheads wherever possible. Techniques such as quality management and careful monitoring of the costs of quality can also aid this process.

Low-Cost Suppliers

Utilizing low-cost suppliers, perhaps from overseas suppliers where labor costs may be lower can also not only keep cost low but provide a competitive advantage. This, however, is only an advantage to the extent that competitor organizations do not adopt the same policy. Movements in the exchange rates can undermine this advantage if it is not possible to pass on cost increases to customers.

Location

The choice of location can also be a source of a cost advantage. For example, locating the operations in a less expensive area such as an out-of-town location, or where government grants are available. There could be a trade-off in the cost of production versus transportation costs if the production is undertaken at a distance from the market. The most advantageous scenario is where low-cost production can be undertaken close to the markets served.

Differentiation

Differentiation is providing a product or service that is significantly different to the competitor offering and the difference is valued by and effectively communicated to the customer. Competitive advantage is gained through the particular characteristics of an organization's products that satisfy customer needs more directly or better than the competitors. As with cost leadership there are several techniques that can be used to aid a strategy of differentiation.

Strong Brand Image

The development of a strong brand image can help to create a barrier to entry as it takes time and money to develop the brand. New products and product variations can be developed from a strong corporate or product brand. In today's environment, taking care not to damage the corporate brand is a significant factor in maintaining the corporate image, especially in the context of corporate scandals or celebrity endorsements. Indeed accounting scandals of late, such as accounting fraud or tax avoidance, can impact on an organization's brand. Thus, the accountant has a role to play in maintaining the corporate image.

Features and Functionality

Developing features and functionality that provide the differentiating factor can provide a competitive advantage. A key element here is that the differentiating factor must be valued by the customer to support a higher price. Techniques such as value engineering and target costing can be utilized to help develop viable products that have distinctive features to the competition. There is a danger that in poor economic conditions, such as a recession, demand for differentiated products may reduce as consumers switch to the low-cost products.

Product Augmentation

A strategy that is followed by many organizations in today's customer service-led economy is to augment the product offering to provide additional elements such as after sales support. Techniques such as the analysis of the value system can be utilized to help determine where value can be added to the customer.

Value System

Elements of the value system such as information technology development or human resource management can be utilized to create new products or service elements, for example, enhanced customer service, flexibility to customer demands creating the ability to customize products. As with cost leadership new technologies available can provide competitors with the ability to erode this advantage.

Effective Marketing Campaigns

The consumer markets are becoming more sophisticated and the differentiating features of a product need to be clearly communicated to consumers, so the product needs to be backed up by effective marketing, but equally the product has to back the marketing. Consumers are quick to spot that the product does not live up to the marketing claims with a resultant reduction in the credibility of the brand.

Focus (or Niche) Strategy

In a focus strategy, an organization concentrates its attention on one or more particular segments or niche markets, and does not try to serve the entire market with a single product. Information technology can be useful in establishing the exact determining characteristics of the chosen niche, using existing customer records. For example, an analysis of the customer base using customer profitability analysis may indicate a highly profitable segment in which the organization has a competitive advantage and therefore the adoption of a focus strategy may be beneficial. A focus strategy is often said to be adopted by organizations that lack the resources to service the total market. It can, however, be a conscious decision to focus on a segment, or segments, of the market regardless of resources available, if this is a more profitable strategy. The focus of the strategy can be on cost or differentiation.

(a) A cost-focus strategy aims to be a cost leader for a particular segment.
(b) A differentiation-focus strategy pursues differentiation for a chosen segment.

There are several advantages to adopting a focus strategy.

Focus on Customer Type

The organization is able to focus its resources on satisfying the needs of a particular customer type and thus does not necessarily spread itself too thinly by trying to satisfy a range of customer needs. A difficulty here is that the organization is limited somewhat by the growth in the market segment. This emphasizes the need to monitor changes in the environment.

Niche Market Operation

An organization that dominates a niche market is able to reduce the amount of competition to which it is exposed. Technology changes can undermine this advantage by enabling the production of small volumes at a lower cost, or providing the service more speedily. For example, on-demand printing made low-volume and specialist books a viable option for both large and small organizations.

Table 5.1 provides examples of competitive strategies and the techniques employed to support them.

Table 5.1 Examples of competitive strategies

Cost leadership	
Walmart	Everyday low prices to attract customers Large-scale and efficient supply chains High volumes and economies of scale
McDonald's	Standard processes Division of labor Centralized purchasing
IKEA	Sourcing of products in low-wage countries Very basic level of service, little after-sales service provision
Low-cost airlines such as TWA, Jetstar	No-frills travel Quick turnaround
Differentiation	
Apple	Technology advantage User interface
Mercedes-Benz	Prestige vehicle Quality image Precision engineering
Nike	Association with successful sports personalities Range of specialist shoes and clothing High-profile brand
Focus	
Oscar Health Insurance	Focuses on the New York market only Uses a slogan of "No more referrals" Allows customers to talk to doctor to tailor quote
Whole Foods	Focuses on local stores taking away feeling of big store image Promotes "greener" lifestyle

The Danger of Being Stuck in the Middle

During the 1980s when Porter developed his model of generic competitive strategies it could be said that there were organizations that were definite cost leaders and those that were differentiators. Porter argued that it is dangerous to be "stuck in the middle." This is illustrated in Figure 5.1.

The cost leader offers a basic product at low cost and charges a price that provides a reasonable and sustainable profit. The differentiator has a higher cost base due to offering additional features or service elements but, as these are valued by the customer, the differentiator is able to charge a higher price to produce a sustainable profit level. Suppose a competitor

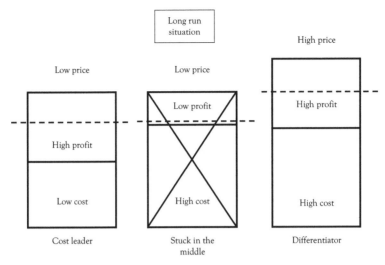

Figure 5.1 The danger of being stuck in the middle

enters the market offering the same product or service as the differentiator, and therefore has the same costs. The strategy of the new entrant is to match the price of the low-cost provider, thus providing a lower profit. This could be successful in the short term as the competitor in the middle will attract customers from both the cost leader and the differentiator. In the long term, however, both the cost leader and the differentiator will react and reduce prices. The customers of the differentiator will revert back to the original, probably due to the established nature of the brand name. The stuck in the middle competitor will need to respond by reducing its price to the cost leader to which it had aligned its pricing strategy on entry to the market. The profitability of the stuck in the middle is now not sustainable and it is likely that the organization will fail. Therefore, in a competitive market being stuck in the middle is not a sustainable strategy in the long term.

This explanation works for the markets in the 1980s when it was clear that there were cost-led and quality-led producers. However, it could be argued that today's consumer is more sophisticated and expects even the value for money products to be of good quality, which makes it more difficult to differentiate purely on the grounds of quality. Most organizations today utilize marketing techniques to try and convince the consumer that their product or service is better, or different, than the competition and it is probably true that all organizations are trying to keep costs to a minimum. Therefore to the casual observer it often becomes blurred as to whether the company is actually competing on cost or differentiation. The strategy of Heinz is to put products in cans for as little money as possible, but Heinz used marketing to convince the consumer that "Beans means Heinz." Porter's message in the 1980s was that it is important for organizations to be clear about what their strategy is and not to become sidetracked to find themselves stuck in the middle with no clear strategy. It could be said that organizations that provide good quality products at low cost are stuck in the middle but, if this is the conscious decision and management are clear about the strategy, then in essence there is nothing wrong with this approach. Organizations in this situation may be, as some well-known supermarkets profess, striving to be a cost leader in a quality, value-added market. These markets, such as food retailing, are characterized as being highly competitive with a range of organizations that span low-cost budget providers at one end of the market to organizations that are clearly targeting a more discerning customer prepared to pay a high price for high quality, and those in the middle. These markets can support a range of competitor organizations but are often low-margin businesses reliant on market share for their profitability.

The Value Creation System Revisited

One of the key elements for the success of an organization today is the development of a sustainable competitive advantage. Ideally that advantage needs to be unique, sustainable, and valued by and relevant to the customer. The difficult element today is the sustainability aspect. The internal analysis can aid the development of the competitive advantage, as a detailed analysis of the strengths and weaknesses relative to the competition can help to establish not only a core competence but also a distinctive competence that the competitive advantage can be built around. A core competence can be described as an activity that the organization needs to be good at in order to survive in the industry, whereas the distinctive competence is an activity at which the organization excels to a greater degree than its competitor organizations. In Chapter 3 the analysis of the value creation system was put forward as a useful tool to aid the development of a competitive advantage. The value creation system can also be utilized to support the strategies of cost leadership and differentiation.

Configuring the value creation system to support the strategy is a critical part of sustaining a competitive advantage. The competitive strategy should also be sustainable through the external value system or supply chain. It is therefore significant in supplier evaluation and also customer profitability analysis, and not just in business-to-business markets, but also in consumer markets where the customer adds value, such as the do-it-yourself (DIY) market or flat-pack furniture. It is important to ensure that the competitive strategy is consistent throughout the entirety of the supply chain.

The importance of information flows within the value system should not be understated as these can be as important as physical flows of products, for example, flows of information from the customer to the suppliers or partner organizations. Retailers who sell a washing machine and arrange for a local plumber to install it at the customer's convenience need to make sure that it is a profitable enterprise for all parties. Therefore the availability of cost information through the supply chain can be important. The provision of complementary services is becoming more significant in the complex supply chains developing in today's business environment.

It was noted in Chapter 3 during the discussion of the internal analysis that activity-based costing (ABC) can be utilized within the value system to identify costs of activities and support the competitive strategy. ABC can aid the support of a cost leadership strategy by assisting in the management of costs that are critical in the provision of the product or service. Similarly, as a differentiation strategy might be concerned with providing a higher quality or increased value added, enabling a higher price to be charged, ABC can again assist in the management of the critical activities.

Activity-Based Costing (ABC)

In order to arrive at a full product cost the overhead costs need to be allocated to products. Traditionally overheads might have been allocated to products on a single companywide basis, such as labor hours, machine hours, material kilograms used, or simply based on the number of units produced. In more sophisticated forms various categories of overheads would be allocated to products on the most appropriate basis. For example warehousing costs might be allocated on the square meter of space occupied.

An overhead absorption rate based on labor hours would be calculated as follows:

$$\frac{\text{Total overhead costs}}{\text{Total labor hours}} = \text{Overhead rate per labor hour}$$

$$\frac{\$400,000}{200,000} = \$2 \text{ per labor hour}$$

The cost of a product would then be calculated as shown in Table 5.2.

When overheads are allocated using a single absorption rate, for example direct labor hours, the effect could be to penalize those products that utilize a high amount of labor; or if allocated on a machine basis it penalizes products that are machine-intensive. The danger is that, depending on the basis used, different cost allocations could arise and encourage an incorrect decision.

ABC is a method of allocating overheads to products using multiple bases on which to allocate the costs to products. It is said that activities create costs and therefore the logical way to allocate costs to products is via the activities that are undertaken to create and provide the products or services. This is one reason why ABC fits well with the analysis of the value creation system in determining and sustaining a competitive advantage as both are concerned with identifying activities that add value.

As ABC uses a range of different bases, more appropriate and directly aligned to the activity that creates the cost, it is said to produce a fairer

Table 5.2 Calculation of product cost

		$
Materials	2 kg @ $2 per kg	4
Labor	1 hour @ $12 per hour	12
Total direct costs		16
Overhead costs	1 labor hour @ $2	2
Total cost		18

allocation of overhead costs. It has the added benefit of highlighting the cost of activities that could stimulate management action. The banking industry was allegedly shocked to realize how much it cost to process a check when ABC was applied.

The technique tends to be more appropriate to industries that have high fixed overhead costs but that undertake a range of activities, such as banking, universities, and hospitals. It is worth noting that when implementing ABC the volume of information and data required about activities, as well as costs, increases. Modern information systems, however, ease the burden of collecting information about activities as they are capable of collecting nonfinancial and financial data in a common database that can then be analyzed across products.

Ideally costs and activities should be based on forecast/estimated (budgeted) levels of activity as there is no guarantee that using historical data will be an accurate representation of the costs and activities of the next year. Therefore, as with all cost systems based on forecast data, the accuracy will depend on the degree of accuracy that can be applied to the forecasts. It can be utilized as a target-setting process, that is, setting targets for costs, and then monitoring against these so that experience is built up over time, which results in more accurate forecasts. As with most aspects of planning the better the understanding, the better the plan.

The Process of ABC—an Example

ABC Inc. is considering producing a range of picnic tables. The accountant has been asked for input to the pricing decision. The following information shown in Table 5.3 has been collected.

Table 5.3 Overhead costs analyzed by cost pool

Activity	Cost driver (basis of allocation)	Cost pool ($)
Assembly	Number of labor hours	55,998
Purchasing department	Number of purchase orders	1,989
Delivery costs	Number of deliveries	30,000
Machine maintenance	Number of machine hours	46,500
Inspection and quality and control	Number of inspections	25,000
Total overhead costs		159,487

There are three styles of table proposed: round, square, and octagon. Information relating to the production process is shown in Table 5.4. Labor is paid at $10 per hour including social charges.

The ABC Process

The total activity level is calculated for each activity using the information in Table 5.4 and, using the cost pool information in Table 5.3, a rate per activity is calculated. This creates a cost driver rate per activity as shown in Table 5.5

Table 5.4 Product information for ABC

	Round	Square	Octagon
Direct material costs per unit	$120	$105	$115
Number of machine hours required per individual product	0.75 hour	0.5 hour	1.0 hour
Number of labor hours required per individual product	2 hours	2 hours	2.1 hours
Number of purchase orders received from central purchasing	3	4	6
Number of deliveries made to central warehouse	10	30	40
Number of inspections	150	150	200
Production (number of units)	1,500	1,500	2,000
Markup on cost to be applied	30%	30%	40%

Table 5.5 Cost driver rate per activity

Rate per cost driver			
	$	Total activity	Activity rate ($)
Assembly—activity of labor hours	55,998	10,200	5.49
Purchasing—activity of purchases	1,989	13	153.00
Delivery—activity of deliveries	30,000	80	375.00
Machine maintenance—activity of machine hours	46,500	3,875	12.00
Inspection—activity of inspections	25,000	500	50.00
Total	159,487		

Table 5.6 Overhead rate per product

	Round	Square	Octagon	Total
	$	$	$	$
Assembly	16,470	16,470	23,058	55,998
Purchasing	459	612	918	1,989
Delivery	3,750	11,250	15,000	30,000
Machine maintenance	13,500	9,000	24,000	46,500
Inspection	7,500	7,500	10,000	25,000
Total overheads per product	41,679	44,832	72,976	159,487
Production units	1,500	1,500	2,000	
Overhead rate per product ($)	27.79	29.89	36.49	

Table 5.7 Calculation of selling price per product

Product cost and selling price using ABC			
	Round	Square	Octagon
	$	$	$
Materials	120.00	105.00	115.00
Labor	20.00	20.00	21.00
Overheads	27.79	29.89	36.49
Total cost	167.79	154.89	172.49
Markup	50.34	46.47	69.00
Selling price	218.13	201.36	241.49

Calculate the overheads assigned to each product by multiplying the activity per product by the cost driver rates and ascertain the overhead cost per product. The result of this step is shown in Table 5.6.

Finally we can calculate cost and selling price using ABC. This is shown in Table 5.7.

Benefits of ABC

The use of multiple rates based on the actual activities provides a fairer allocation of overheads associated with each product, as it takes account of the use made of various activities. For example, Octagon uses more inspection resources and therefore is charged more of the cost incurred for inspection. The ABC method also highlights the costs of handling orders and delivery as well as inspection and these areas could be targeted for further investigation. For example, there may be more efficient ways of operation, or allocation of resources, that could potentially reduce the costs of these activities improving the profitability of all products. In this way ABC supports the maintenance of a cost leadership strategy.

It is also worth noting that with ABC if the level of activity changes on the delivery, order handling, and inspections then the allocation of costs would also change. It can be dangerous to put too much emphasis on the accuracy of ABC costs, as if they are based on previous years, then these are only valid if the activity in the next year is similar. Also, if based on estimates of next year's activity they rely on the degree of accuracy in the estimated activity. ABC provides more detailed information on which to make an informed pricing decision but consideration should also be given to other factors such as market price, complementary products, degree of marketing support, production capacity, and the overall pricing objective. It is important to discuss the figures with the marketing department, as well as production, and undertaking some sensitivity analysis around the volumes, as pricing decisions can change the mix of products sold, which in turn will influence the level of activity such as order handling and delivery, thus affecting the ABC costs.

ABC can also aid the maintenance of a differentiation strategy by providing a more informed cost associated with the functionality or service elements provided as part of the product/service offering. This can be invaluable not only in determining the pricing strategy but also in evaluating the value added to the end product in real terms. Differentiators invariably have a higher cost base and therefore understanding the costs of the differentiation factors is significant for the sustainability of the strategy in a competitive market.

Activity-Based Management (ABM)

When considering ABC it is worth noting that undertaking an ABC exercise achieves nothing if not followed up by management action. It is therefore necessary to implement activity-based management systems at the same time. ABM and ABC go together as ABM is concerned with the management of activities to improve the performance of the organization. ABC effectively puts a cost on these activities. ABM is also effective if utilized in conjunction with the analysis of the value creation system in that the organization is able to actively manage the activities. This is a requirement of sustaining a competitive advantage. The value system facilitates the identification of a competitive advantage, while ABM can facilitate the management of the activities to sustain the advantage. ABC provides information that can aid the identification of areas where costs need further investigation as well as valuable information that can feed into pricing strategies, make or buy, and outsourcing decisions.

Cost of Quality

Control of quality is often a key element in a differentiation strategy. Therefore understanding the costs associated with quality is an important aspect of the sustainability of the strategy. Quality has many different definitions but perhaps the one best suited to the purpose of this book is that quality means "fitness for purpose," that is, does the product or service do what it is supposed to do? This then means that even low-cost items are subject to the costs of quality.

The Costs of Quality Can Be Analyzed into Four Main Categories

- Prevention—expenditures incurred to keep quality defects from occurring. These are typically costs such as training, supplier evaluation, and quality planning.
- Appraisal—costs incurred to identify and control if the products or services conform to the required specification. These are typically costs of inspection, quality control, supplier monitoring, and customer surveys.
- Internal failure—any costs incurred as a result of failures identified via the appraisal system before the delivery to the customer. These are typically costs of reworking, downtime, equipment failure, reinspection, and testing.
- External failure—costs incurred to rectify quality defects after the product or service has been delivered or provided to the

customer. These are typically warranty costs, product liability insurance schemes, and contribution lost from customers who do not return, or who do not consider the offering due to loss of corporate reputation.

These can be separated into conformity and nonconformity as shown in Table 5.8

Most organizations will have some form of costs of conformity that can be budgeted for. Objectives can be set to reduce or keep to a minimum the costs of conformity. Ideally, if nothing ever went wrong, the cost of nonconformity should be zero. However, it can be seen that if things do go wrong then there is a cost associated with the failure. Costs of rectification either before or after the customer receives the product or service will be incurred and, in the case of external failure, it could result in loss of reputation and potentially future sales. The cost in this case is the lost contribution on those sales.

It is not just a case of monitoring the costs but of understanding the costs of quality and making decisions about the potential trade-off between costs. This can impact on the marketing offering. For example, an organization may decide to reduce the number of inspections based on statistical analysis that historically very few products are manufactured that are of poor quality. This, however, increases the potential risk that a defective product could get through the process and into the hands of the customer. The policy could then be to replace the product immediately, free of charge and without question. The customer focuses on the excellent customer service rather than the fact that there was a problem. The organization can also make trade-offs in terms of training and inspection. If the investment in training is increased, in theory the number of failures should be reduced and the cost of failure should also be reduced or eliminated. In this way it can be seen that accounting for the costs of quality

Table 5.8 *Costs of conformity and costs of nonconformity*

Cost of conformity	Cost of nonconformity
• Prevention costs • Appraisal costs	• Internal failure costs • External failure costs

is not just a monitoring activity but can form the basis of policy decisions and support the competitive strategy.

Costs of Quality Report

A typical example of a costs of quality report is shown in Table 5.9.

Table 5.9 A typical costs of quality report

	20x1	20x0	Change
	$	$	%
Prevention costs			
Training	16,000	15,000	7
Quality planning	5,000	5,200	−4
Supplier evaluation	2,000	3,000	−33
Other quality improvements	4,500	6,000	−25
Total prevention costs	27,500	29,200	−6
Appraisal costs			
Testing	50,000	51,500	−3
Inspection	40,000	42,000	−5
Supplier monitoring	10,000	11,000	−9
Customer surveys	12,000	10,000	20
Total appraisal costs	112,000	114,500	−2
Internal failure costs			
Rework and rejects	7,500	8,000	−6
Reinspection and testing	3,000	2,500	20
Equipment failure cost of repairs	1,500	1,500	0
Downtime	1,000	1,200	−17
Total internal failure costs	13,000	13,200	−2
External failure costs			
Product liability costs	75,000	75,000	0
Repairs under warranty	120,000	125,000	−4
Contribution foregone from lost sales	15,000	13,000	15
Total external failure costs	210,000	213,000	−1
Total cost of quality	362,500	369,900	−2

Management Accounting in Support of the Competitive Strategies

Appropriate Accounting Techniques

Ensuring that the appropriate accounting techniques and reporting enables management to control costs in support of the cost leadership strategy. These can include techniques such as ABC to highlight activities where business processes could be improved to reduce costs.

Monitoring and Reporting

Monitoring and reporting on the costs of quality to support a cost leadership strategy and also one of differentiation, particularly if the differentiation factor is based on high-quality products.

Sustainability of Competitive Strategy

Coupled with the environmental analysis evaluating whether the competitive strategy is viable in the long run. For example, if the market is becoming highly competitive and margins are being reduced due to downward pressure on prices, a cost-led strategy may not be viable in the long run if economies of scale cannot be maintained.

Evaluation of Options

Assisting in the decision to pursue a strategic option by assessing the likely outcomes in financial terms based on the use of strategic tools. For example, evaluating competitive strategies to attract profitable customers (CPA), by developing new products for growing markets (portfolio analysis), given the changes in the environment and the current position relative to the key competitors. The accountant is able to utilize the analysis of several models and tools by converting them to the common language of financial numbers.

CHAPTER 6

Strategic Options Generation

Ansoff's Growth Vector Matrix

Ansoff's (1965) growth vector matrix describes how a combination of an organization's activities in existing and new markets with existing and new products can lead to growth. It provides a useful framework for thinking about potential strategic options available to an organization. If a gap has been identified as a result of the SWOT analysis the various growth strategies shown in Figure 6.1, provides a good basis for ways to fill the gap.

The strategies indicated on the matrix are not the only strategic options available to an organization but they represent ways in which an organization may seek to grow its business. Strategies can also consist of more than one element, for example, an organization may pursue a dual strategy of product development and market development. It is also possible to launch a new product or enter a new market using a strategy of market penetration; therefore, the strategies can be used in conjunction with one another.

Strategies for Growth

Withdrawal

Portfolio analysis was discussed in Chapter 3 in which the possibility of withdrawing an existing product from the market was highlighted as an option. This can be a way of releasing resources that can be diverted to more profitable products and therefore presents itself as an option to support growth. In a similar way, withdrawing from unprofitable markets can achieve the same objective of releasing valuable resources.

Market Penetration

Market penetration refers to the situation where an organization seeks to increase its market share in existing markets with the existing products, for example, through competitive pricing, advertising, sales promotion,

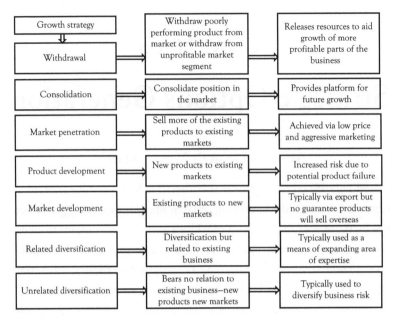

Figure 6.1 Growth strategies to fill the profits gap

and so on. The strategy seeks to secure dominance in growth markets. Models such as portfolio analysis could be utilized to identify potential markets where this strategy might be appropriate to develop a question mark product into a star product. Market penetration can also be used to force out competition from the market leaving the organization with a dominate market share. Typical strategies employ price and product awareness where a discounted price is offered coupled with aggressive marketing campaigns. The impact on margins needs to be considered here as there is a danger that if an aggressive pricing strategy is employed to achieve the market dominance it could reduce the overall profitability of the market, as consumers become used to the lower price. Marketing devices employed to encourage brand loyalty such as the introduction of loyalty cards and promotional activity are also relevant, but again the cost of providing these needs to be understood.

Consolidation

Consolidation refers to the situation where a company seeks to consolidate its position within a market by maintaining its market share. Customer loyalty programs are common techniques. Focusing more effort on the profitable market segments determined via customer profitability analysis or on markets where a market leading position can be maintained are common strategies that can be employed to consolidate the organization's position in the market.

Product Development

Product development refers to developing new products to existing customers. It is slightly riskier than concentrating on existing products and existing markets, as not all new products will be successful. The argument is that the organization should understand its customers very well and therefore be able to launch products that are attractive to existing markets. Ideally they should be new products to the profitable customers. It is also relatively important to keep a product base up to date via the development of the new product offerings, particularly if cash cows are reaching the end of their life. If this is maintained as a long-term strategy it requires constant investment, for example, in technology industries such as mobile phones. The technology development required to maintain a market lead requires a continuous investment in new products linked to advertising to persuade customers to upgrade to the new products.

Market Development

Market development refers to the strategy of entering new markets with existing products and is also riskier than market penetration and consolidation as the products may not sell well in new markets. It can include new geographical areas and new channels to market, such as selling via the Internet or cable TV shopping channels. The classic example is expanding sales into overseas markets, which raises cultural issues and may require some adjustment to the product offering with an associated impact on costs, pricing, and profitability.

Diversification

Diversification is essentially selling new products into new markets and represents the option with the greatest risk to the company. Diversification may be a suitable strategy if existing markets are becoming very competitive or are changing rapidly, thus it may help to spread the risk for the organization. Diversification can be subdivided into related and unrelated. Related diversification has some relationship to existing activities, whereas unrelated diversification is something completely new, and can represent a greater risk.

A Mix of Strategic Options for Growth

In the mid-1980s British Telecom enjoyed a near monopoly position in the infrastructure telecoms market in the United Kingdom. The industry regulator decided to change this situation as it was deemed to be anticompetitive. However, BT found that the domestic market was mature and growing very slowly, if at all. However, at the same time there was increasing de-regulation in other areas of the world and markets such as Africa and Asia were showing signs of strong growth. The senior management of BT were looking to diversify their interests into media and develop new products that could be offered via the provision of superfast broadband. As a strategy they sought to consolidate their position in their domestic market for telecoms provision while using a strategy of market penetration to target expansion in the growing overseas markets. A BT Sports TV channel was launched with the acquisition of rights to broadcast premier sporting events. The management therefore adopted several of the strategies outlined in this section to develop an overall strategy sufficient to close the profits gap.

Pricing Policy

Both product and market development have implications for pricing. When thinking about pricing it is important to understand the pricing objective. For example, is the objective to achieve volume sales, for example, market penetration, or to maximize profits? These indicate a low price or high price, respectively. Pricing could also be determined by reference to the three Cs: cost, which is the lowest price an organization would ideally wish to set, unless adopting a loss leader approach;

Table 6.1 Pricing strategy

	Low level of marketing relying on word of mouth	High level of marketing spend
Low price	Slow penetration	Rapid penetration
High price	Slow skimming	Rapid skimming

customer-perceived price, which is the price that customers would be prepared to pay determined by marketing research; or competitor pricing in which the price is set at the level of a competitor where competition is focused on product rather than price.

There is also a link between pricing and marketing, which is illustrated in Table 6.1.

The choice can be to penetrate the market or skim profit off the market before competitors follow. This is particularly relevant to new product development. There are also implications for manufacturing, as discussed in Chapter 3 under the product life cycle, where a decision has to be made concerning the level of production and initial inventory levels. This provides another example of where the techniques discussed are not used in isolation but are relevant to many different stages of strategy development and implementation, hence supporting the strategic management process.

Evaluating Viable International Markets

The first step in overseas expansion is usually exporting. This can be achieved by the organization selling directly to customers, or via an overseas agent. Understanding demand conditions is a key factor in deciding whether exporting is a potential opportunity. The next step might be to open a sales office in the country. If the market proves to be extremely promising production often follows the sales. In cases where establishing a production capability in the country is being considered the availability of factors such as land, labor, capital, education, technology, and infrastructure needs to be evaluated. The costs of progression and the viability of the options are an area where the accountant is well placed to support the strategic decision.

Target Costing

Target costing is a technique that can be used to test whether a product or service is a viable option. The target cost is calculated as follows:

$$\text{Market price} - \text{required profit margin} = \text{target cost}$$

The market price would be determined by the marketing team and can be defined as: what would consumers be prepared to pay for a product or service such as this? If there is already a competitor product in the market it may be determined from competitor pricing, or as suggested by the formula the market price. If the desired profit margin is then deducted the target cost is derived. If the target cost cannot be reached then it could be argued that the product or service is not a viable option. The basic concept is that the project team could look at the product features, manufacturing process, distribution options, marketing channels, and so on, to see if cost savings can be made to reach the target cost. The accountant would work as part of team that would include other professionals such as designers, operations, and marketing personnel to explore ways of making a product that is financially viable and appealing to customers. In large organizations much of this work might be undertaken by design teams, but in medium to small organizations the accountant can be heavily involved in the process. Activity-based costing and analysis of the value system can be utilized, as well as other design techniques outside the scope of this book, but the significance of pricing and cost decisions cannot be underestimated within the strategy formulation and implementation phases.

Life Cycle Costing

The product life cycle described in Chapter 3 primarily focused on the life of the product from launch to decline, that is, the sales product life. However, products begin much earlier and there are many decisions to make before the final decision to launch is made. The new product development process will include a business case in which a financial analysis will form a key part of the justification. It is also important to realize that once the product is launched many cost decisions have been locked in, or committed too, earlier in the process. A high proportion of costs are actually committed at the design stage that will only be incurred during the manufacturing stage and beyond, for example, material costs and ease of repair or maintenance. Therefore it is important to realize the impact this may have on the product's profitability later in the life cycle. Product costs should be considered throughout the entirety of the product life at the beginning, which avoids surprises later in the process, for example, a beautiful design that proves very expensive to manufacture. The accountant needs to work with functional specialists to be able to gather information on costs incurred throughout the whole of the life cycle.

The issue of sustainability is also highly relevant today and it is suggested that the life cycle costs should extend to include the cost of disposal after use, cradle to grave, or the cost of recycling the product into another product, termed cradle to cradle. The responsibility for recycling has implications for pricing as, if manufacturers are responsible, it will be desirable to seek to recover the cost of this within the price. Therefore, it is important to understand the total cost, including the cost of recycling, in order to determine whether this cost can be passed on to the customer. This is an issue that organizations will need to monitor via environmental analysis as many governments are beginning to legislate to make manufacturers responsible for the recycling of elements of the products, or to ensure that products are capable of being recycled. The search for new sustainable material sources that are financially viable can be another area where accountants are able to work with other professionals within the organization.

Methods of Growth

The strategic options available to an organization can be viewed as a three-stage process. Review the competitive strategy (Chapter 5) for appropriateness given the changes in the environment, decide the strategic option to be undertaken based on Ansoff's ideas, and then determine the best method of achieving the strategy. This could be achieved via organic growth, that is, undertaking the strategy by relying on the organization's own resources and capabilities, merger or acquisition, or joint development. This section briefly considers the benefits and drawbacks of each method before looking at the accountant's role.

Organic Growth/Internal Development

Organic growth involves developing the internal resources and capabilities of the organization. The obvious advantage is that the organization is in total control over its own destiny and has strategic independence. The organization does not have to compromise on its strategic plans, but conversely it is bearing all of the risk and costs of development. The process of developing new products and new markets under an organization's own resources can take a prolonged period of time, involve considerable investment in resources, and carry a high risk. However, it is possible to spread the investment over a period of time and the organization is gaining experience and enhancing its capabilities via organizational learning through direct involvement in the process of developing new products and markets.

Mergers and Acquisitions

The option of a merger or acquisition provides a speedier option in many instances than organic development. Entry into new markets or acquiring new products to complement an existing product portfolio can be achieved via merger or acquisition. The strengthening of a poorly balanced product portfolio, as determined by portfolio analysis, could be improved. For example a merger between two pharmaceutical companies where one has many profitable products but no new products in development, and the other has products in development but very few cash cows would benefit both companies by producing a merged company with a balanced portfolio of products. New capabilities and knowledge can be acquired such as expertise in technology, or enhanced skill base. Local knowledge of markets can be gained or the strategy can be utilized as a means of overcoming barriers to entry to overseas markets, perhaps by merging with a local organization already operating in the country. Financial benefits can arise from mergers, such as improved financial efficiency via a stronger balance sheet, or achieving tax efficiencies due to tax treaties between different tax regimes where the companies are based in different countries. Rationalizing product capacity or releasing value by selling off unprofitable parts could also be a motivation for merger and acquisition activity. There are, however, some drawbacks such as the potential for a clash of cultures. This is more in evidence as the two organizations try to find a way to integrate the operations and potential rationalization costs, such as the elimination of duplicated resources, or excess capacity is closed down involving redundancy of personnel.

Factors that need to be considered when undertaking an acquisition or merger include:

- Strategic fit—does it build on the strengths, address the weaknesses, grasp the opportunities, or help to minimize the threats?
- Financing—how will the acquisition be financed? What level of financial risk is involved?
- Stakeholders' attitude, particularly shareholders—what do the stakeholders involved think of the proposed acquisition or merger? Are they for or against? How will they be affected?
- Value of the target—how to value the potential target? What is the ideal price? What is the maximum that the organization is prepared to pay? That is, what are the boundaries for negotiation?
- Effect on other organizations—what is the impact on suppliers, customers, and intermediaries?
- Rationalization costs, both financial and human—what are the costs of integration and how will these be managed? How will the impact on employees of both organizations be managed?
- Potential synergies—what are the benefits of acquisition or merger in terms of synergies? Operating, marketing, and administrative synergies all need to be considered to ensure that they are actually achieved.
- The manner of integration and management approach—how much autonomy will be allowed to the acquired or merged organization(s)?

Integration Issues

The manner of integration of an acquisition can range from leaving the organization completely autonomous to subsuming the organization into the operations of the acquiring organization. This process needs careful consideration as it has implications for motivation of staff and the effectiveness and costs of the integration. The parent organization also needs to consider the degree of control that it grants to a newly acquired subsidiary or business unit. The choices here are:

- Financial control in which the parent organization allows a high degree of autonomy but sets strong financial controls.
- Strategic planning in which the parent organization undertakes the planning for the subsidiary and management simply implement the plan.
- Strategic control is a halfway house in which the parent sets strategic guidelines within which the subsidiary has some autonomy. This is sometimes referred to as parental control.

Joint Development Forms

Consortia

Consortia in which a number of individual organizations join together for the purposes of undertaking a large-scale project, for example, a large-scale construction project.

Joint Venture

Joint venture, or equity alliance, in which a separate legal entity is formed to pursue a common purpose. The participant organizations still exist in their own right and the joint venture is a separate legal entity that employs its own staff. Profits and losses are shared in accordance with a joint venture agreement as is the provision of resources and operational aspects of the venture. The key benefits here are that costs and risks can be shared as well as expertise, but there is the potential for disagreement between partners, or worse the failure of one partner organization. Compromises might also need to be made to accommodate partner views resulting in a dilution of the strategic aims and objectives.

Strategic Alliance

A nonequity strategic alliance is usually governed by a contractual arrangement, which benefits both parties. Typical examples might be a franchise arrangement in which the franchisor grants certain rights to the franchisees, and provides the product or know-how and training, thus retaining some control over quality as well as managing the brand image and marketing. The franchisee contributes personal commitment to success, capital, and often local knowledge.

Licensing

There are also licensing agreements whereby the organization grants rights to manufacture a product under license, or confers rights to use a product, process, or brand name for which the licensee pays a royalty payment or fee.

Local Agent

In the case of overseas developments the use of local agents is often beneficial as they provide the local knowledge of the market and regulatory regimes of operating in the country. They can be incentivized to encourage referrals with penalties also imposed to prevent misuse of the arrangement.

De-Merger

An option that should not be overlooked is that of de-merger where an organization decides to split into several smaller parts to become more focused on specific markets, or to achieve more flexibility and speed of response to environmental changes from a smaller-scale operation.

Unprofitable parts or elements of the business can also be sold off where there is no longer a strategic fit with the overall direction of the organization.

Management Accounting in Support of Strategic Options Generation

Withdrawal Options

Working with marketing personnel to identify candidates for withdrawal of products from markets or withdrawing operations from unprofitable markets. The use of portfolio analysis and customer profitability analysis can be helpful here.

Pricing Decisions

Assisting in the pricing decision via costing and pricing strategies. This is particularly useful in market penetration strategies where a loss leader approach might be adopted, as the potential cost of such a strategy needs careful consideration. Similarly the use of price and product awareness strategies needs careful evaluation prior to implementation.

New Markets

Evaluation of potential new markets and methods of entry in terms of the costs of acquiring the necessary resources and access options to the market.

Costing New Products

The use of target costing and life cycle costing methods to understand the costs of product development and evaluating the potential viability of product development strategies, as well as contributing to the business case or, indeed, assessing the validity of a business case. ABC can also aid the achievement of target costs by highlighting costly activities. Benchmarking exercises can also be employed to improve the operation of the value creation system.

Methods of Growth

Evaluating the various methods of growth in financial terms, including assisting in the negotiation of joint venture or strategic alliance contractual issues. The accountant could assist the legal team in agreeing the terms of any joint venture by providing detailed financial estimates and allocation of costs.

Investment Appraisal

Utilizing knowledge of investment appraisal techniques, such as net present value calculations (see Chapter 7) and associated sensitivity analysis, in the evaluation of methods of growth, particularly if used as a basis for valuing an acquisition target. The accountant is able to make a significant contribution to the financial aspects of the initial feasibility study as well as the strategic aspects. The overall assessment of the feasibility of the project should include an initial financial appraisal and, at a later stage as more detailed information becomes known and costs and revenue projections become more accurate, updated for known changes. The comparison of actual performance against the plan is also an obvious area for the accountant to be involved—this can aid the learning process for future project appraisals as experience is gained of the option for growth. Knowledge of evaluation techniques and the evaluation of alternative courses of action will be invaluable as the organization makes the final decision. Incorporating risk assessment and sensitivity analysis into the evaluation can also provide valuable information.

Due Diligence

Undertaking financial due diligence of the acquisition target or merger company as well as involvement in the strategic due diligence process.

Forecasting and Monitoring

The provision of estimates and forecasts/budgets as well as establishing monitoring systems and reporting of actual performance is another area where the accountant can make a significant contribution. Generally providing support to nonfinancial managers in the implementation of the strategic option chosen. This does not relate just to the ongoing operations but to the control of initial investment costs and adherence to payment schedules that might be appropriate. Ensuring that the finance is available when required and that the financing of the strategic option chosen is managed effectively.

CHAPTER 7

Strategic Evaluation and Choice

Elements of Strategic Evaluation

The evaluation of options involves the strategic evaluation as well as a financial evaluation.

A useful framework for evaluating strategic options was put forward by Johnson, Scholes, and Whittington (2007) in their book *Exploring Corporate Strategy*. Suitability, acceptability, and feasibility, it is possible to remember this as SAFe. If, however, the aspect of risk is highlighted and considered as a separate element the mnemonic SAFeR can be used.

- Suitability relates to the strategic logic of the strategy. The strategy must fit the company's operational circumstances and strategic capability. It is asking whether the strategy builds on the strengths, addresses the weaknesses, grasps the opportunities, and avoids or minimizes the threats. Does it close any profits gap and is it financially viable?
- Acceptability relates to the stakeholders and as a minimum the key players.
- Feasibility asks whether the strategy can practically be implemented. Is sufficient financing available? Does the organization have or can it acquire the correct resource capability?
- Risk identifies the risk and prompts risk management strategies to manage risk to an acceptable level.

In this chapter we focus on stakeholders, financial viability, and risk management.

Stakeholder Analysis in Relation to Strategic Choices

What Is a Stakeholder and Why Does an Organization Need to Consider Stakeholder Views?

When organizations implement strategies there are many different groups of people who are affected. Therefore it is important for organizations to consider the potential impact that their decisions will have on a range of different stakeholders. Definitions of stakeholders in relation to organizations vary by the emphasis they place on the relationship. In broad terms a stakeholder is any group or individual who is affected by, or can affect, the organization's activities (Freeman 1984). Other authors, such as Clarkson (1995), stress that stakeholders are able to claim ownership rights, or interests in an organization and its activities past, present, or future. These claimed rights or interests are the result of transactions with, or actions taken by, the organization. They may be legal or amoral, individual or collective. Bryson (2004) suggests that stakeholders are persons, groups, or organizations that must somehow be taken into account by leaders, managers and front-line staff. There is broad agreement that stakeholders have an interest or a reliance on the organization and that organizations have a responsibility to their stakeholders. As sustainability is becoming more prominent this leads to the conclusion that stakeholders would include future generations who are not yet born, as organizations need to consider the impact on the planet when making strategic decisions that may impact on sustainability.

Different stakeholder groups will have differing interests and levels of influence in relation to the organization and the decisions that it makes, which indicates why organizations need to assess stakeholder views in relation to the strategy that is adopted. Organizations need to understand the criteria by which stakeholders will judge their performance against their expectations, and therefore what the organizations can do to satisfy those expectations. The degree of power and influence that various stakeholders can exercise, together with the legitimacy of the stakeholder relationship and the urgency of the claim, needs to be taken into account (Mitchell, Agle, and Wood 1997). In reality organizations cannot satisfy all stakeholders and therefore there needs to be a way of identifying and prioritizing those individual or groups that are affected by, or can affect, an organization's ability to achieve its objectives. There will also be an element of trade-off between competing aims and therefore it may be a case of satisfying rather than maximizing stakeholders' needs and expectations.

Classifications of Stakeholders

Stakeholders have varying degrees of interest and influence depending on their relationship to the organization. One approach to deciding which stakeholders are relevant is to view their proximity to the organization in relation to the task or general environment, as illustrated in Figure 7.1. This determines the degree to which the organization relies on the stakeholder group for the successful implementation of its strategies.

Another more simplified and potentially useful way of classifying stakeholders is using the mnemonic ICE, for internal, connected, and external.

Internal

Typically internal stakeholders are often thought of as employees being split between management and workers. However, employees can be broken down into many different groups who will have different interests,

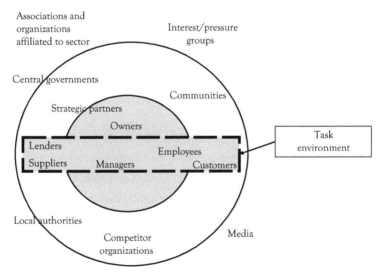

Figure 7.1 Stakeholders in relation to task and general environment

expectations, and degree of power or influence. Consider a hospital in which there are doctors, consultants, administrators, nursing staff, and porters. There may also be groups of workers who are contracted to another organization such as caterers and cleaners. All groups could have a different view or reaction to a strategic decision taken by the organization and some groups may be able to influence the success of the strategy more than others.

Connected

Connected stakeholders have a vested interest in the organization. This will include shareholders and loan providers and sometimes suppliers and customers depending on the strength of the relationship with the organization.

External

External stakeholders might include central government, the general public, pressure groups, and the media.

Like most strategic analysis tools stakeholder analysis is not a precise science. Mendelow (1991) suggested that stakeholders' views will differ depending on the strategic decision being made. There are also different dimensions that need to be considered, such as whether power and influence is individual or collective. For example, an employee or customer may not have much power individually to change a decision, but collectively could exert a higher degree of power, often in the form of a trade union or consumer group. The impact that a stakeholder group may have could also be short term or long term.

It is possible to determine that there will be conflicts arising between stakeholder groups. For example, closing a manufacturing unit will not be acceptable to employees but, if it is increasing profitability via cost reduction and increased efficiency in other units, shareholders may well support the decision. The relative power positions of stakeholder groups can be determined by the degree of dependency an organization has on a stakeholder group at any particular time. For example, an organization that is experiencing serious cash flow problems may be dependent on its bankers to provide it with finance, which puts the bank in a strong position to influence strategy, such that the bank demands a seat on the board of directors in order to protect its position.

The degree of reliance can be analyzed by understanding the degree of disruption, ease of replacement, and degree of uncertainty that a stakeholder group is able to create (Mintzberg 1999). As an example, the London underground train system has a strong driver's union and disputes frequently arise between the union and the management team. The union is in a strong position as a stakeholder as they can disrupt the organization's plans by calling the drivers out on strike, that is, withdrawing their labor. Due to the labor protection laws in the United Kingdom it is difficult to replace employees, certainly in the short term. The union went through a long-running dispute by threatening to go on strike, and then calling it off at the last minute. This created a high level of uncertainty for the thousands of people who use the underground train system to get to work, creating uncertainty in many organizations operating in London. These three factors put the union in a strong position with a high degree of power and influence over the decisions, requiring a participative approach to management by the organization in dealing with the stakeholder group.

Stakeholder Mapping

The technique of stakeholder mapping can be utilized to understand the dynamics of the stakeholder influence on a strategic decision being considered. A typical matrix showing the degree of influence and power on one axis against the expectations or level of interest on the other axis can be used, as shown in Figure 7.2.

Stakeholders with a high degree of power and high degree of interest can be described as key players: strategy must be acceptable to them, at least. These stakeholders can exert considerable influence on the strategic decision under consideration, for example, a major provider of capital such as a bank, or a local authority from whom planning permission is required to develop land. It can extend to powerful suppliers or customers where they hold a high degree of power in negotiations. It is the key players that an organization needs to identify when formulating strategy.

Degree of power and influence

	High	Low
High	These can aid or hinder the implementation of a strategy and need to be involved in the decision making process. They can become the key players in the decision.	These need to be kept informed about the strategic decision, its benefits and impacts, as their cooperation is required to implement the strategy successfully.
Low	These need to be kept satisfied and in some cases an intervention strategy may be required to convince them that the decision is in their interests. These can become key players if their interest level increases.	These need to be monitored in case they become interested or increase their power base, but essentially they can be directed as to what the strategy is and managed accordingly.

Level of interest/ expectations

Figure 7.2 Stakeholder mapping

However, it is important to realize that stakeholders can move from one quadrant to another depending on the situation under review and must therefore be managed appropriately, as indicated in Figure 7.2. Although the analysis can be undertaken as a general exercise, it is best deployed as a way of understanding the key players in relation to a strategic decision.

The Case of Dyson's Decision to Move Production Overseas

Dyson is a UK—based company that became famous for developing a new technology for vacuum cleaners. Soon other products were added to the portfolio. In 2002, the multimillionaire and inventor James Dyson, the owner and then sole shareholder, took the decision to move production of his bagless vacuum cleaners to the Far East with the loss of 800 jobs in the United Kingdom. The decision was also part of the strategy to launch products in the U.S. market as countries such as Malaysia were closer to the U.S. market and the move would not only reduce production costs by 30 percent but also release additional cash that could be used to fund the marketing campaign. James Dyson had been critical of the UK government for not doing enough to support manufacturing,

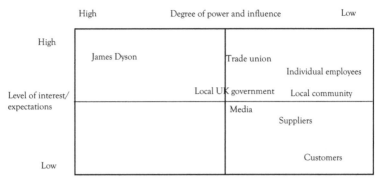

Figure 7.3 Stakeholders affected by the Dyson decision to move production overseas

and not surprisingly the UK government expressed their disappointment at the move. The trade union was also very vocal in their condemnation of the move but could actually do very little to stop the decision. Mapping the stakeholders affected by the decision, as shown in Figure 7.3, illustrates why James Dyson was able to make the decision unopposed as there were no key players with enough power and influence to affect the decision-making process.

Financial Evaluation

The accountant has a key role to play in the evaluation of capital investment and strategic decisions that required significant amounts of investment over a period of time. The term capital investment appraisal is also often referred to as capital budgeting, as the organization may not be able to undertake every investment opportunity, due to a limited availability of capital resources at its disposal. The investment appraisal process therefore provides a basis for evaluating those investments that will enable the organization to close any gap that arises from the GAP analysis discussed in Chapter 4.

It is important to note that strategic decisions should not be based solely on the numerical evaluation but also take account of strategic factors of a nonfinancial nature. There may be circumstances in which it makes sense strategically to undertake a decision that provides benefits other than financial, for example, developing a presence in a geographic

market that eventually opens up access to other markets. This has implications for being sure of the strategic decision being made and the time
frame. For example, establishing a business in Bangladesh can open up
markets in countries such as Northeast India, Nepal, and Bhutan, due
to the strategic importance of their seaports. It may be more appropriate
to evaluate the cost of setting up in Bangladesh as a separate exercise as
the future cash flows emanating from access to other markets may be too
far in the future to be able to estimate with any meaningful accuracy,
even though this may be the real intention behind the strategy. This raises
another important issue in that some strategies, such as the instance of
Bangladesh, can be broken down into phases and at certain points in
the future different decisions can be made. The decision to operate in
Bangladesh can be seen as part of the cost of a much bigger strategy. This
also serves to indicate that an investment appraisal is not just undertaken
once, but the decision should be evaluated at significant milestones to see
if it is still worth continuing given the changes in the environment. There
are therefore exit points or decision points at which the initial decision
can be reassessed in light of new and more up-to-date information.

Methods of Investment Appraisal

Payback Period

A common investment appraisal technique is known as the payback
period. In its simplest form this is answering the question how long does
it take to recoup the initial investment. The technique is easily understood by everyone and the basic principle states that the investment with
the shortest payback period is the preferred option. However, there are
some drawbacks to this method as illustrated in Table 7.1.

Table 7.1 Simple payback period calculation

Years	Project A $	Project B $
0	(1,000)	(1,000)
1	900	100
2	100	900

The immediate difficulty is that both project A and project B payback in two years. However, the natural instinct suggests that project A would be preferred over project B, as more of the investment is recouped in year one. This is instinctively considering two factors: the time value of money, that is, given the choice people would prefer to receive money earlier rather than later as they perceive that the buying power of cash now is more than in the future, owing to inflation and the chance of earning interest, and the risk involved, in that early cash flows represent less risk to their certainty than future cash flows. In its crudest form the payback method can ignore future cash flows received after the payback period. To avoid these problems the technique of discounted cash flows providing a net present value can be utilized instead.

Net Present Value (NPV) Calculation

The net present value (NPV) technique takes account of the time value of money by applying a discount factor to all future cash flows (capital costs and all revenues and expenses) that converts the nominal cash flows into present-day values. It is worth noting that discounted cash flows can be used within the payback method described previously to account for the time value of money. The organization's weighted average cost of capital is typically used as the discount factor, but this can be adjusted to take account of risk and the effect of future financing requirements. This enables a comparison of different investment options that have different timings of cash flow as all cash flows are represented in equivalent values, that is, present-day values. The normal rule is that a project providing a positive NPV would be acceptable in financial terms, and one with a negative NPV would not be acceptable. In the case where there are alternatives the one with the highest positive NPV would be preferred. It is important to reiterate that strategic decisions should not be made purely on the basis of financial evaluation. The example in Table 7.2 illustrates this for three projects, each of which would require an initial investment of $50,000. Each project provides a different profile of net cash flows over the life of the project.

When looking at the nominal cash flow on the left, project B may be preferred as it provides a higher net benefit over the life of the project.

Table 7.2 NPV for three alternative projects

Year	Project A	Project B	Project C	Discount factor (10%)	Project A	Project B	Project C
	Nominal cash flows $,000				Discounted cash flows $,000		
0	(50)	(50)	(50)	1.0	(50)	(50)	(50)
1	28	0	40	0.91	25	0	36
2	22	30	8	0.83	18	25	7
3	8	30	12	0.75	6	22	9
4	4	0	14	0.68	3	0	9
5	0	21	1	0.62	0	13	1
	12	31	25		2	10	12

However, when the timing of the cash flow is considered by applying the discount factor, which converts all cash flows into present-day values, project C produces a higher NPV. This is quite close to project B so a final decision will take into account the nonfinancial factors.

The NPV analysis can be enhanced and made more sophisticated, for example, by applying probability values to future cash flows creating an expected value. The discount factor can be increased over the cost of capital to include a risk factor, and within this different discount rates can be applied to revenues and costs. It may be that costs are more certain than revenue cash flows. This degree of uncertainty can be accommodated by using different discount factors for different items, or inflating costs by an expected rate of inflation and sales by the expected growth in sales value based on volumes and pricing strategy as the market growth is achieved and competitors enter the market.

Internal Rate of Return (IRR)

An internal rate of return can also be calculated as a means of making comparisons. This is the equivalent of the discount factor that is required to achieve a NPV of zero. It can be calculated by trial and error using a NPV calculation with different discount factors until the NPV is zero, or calculated via interpolation using a graphical method of the calculation

Graphical method

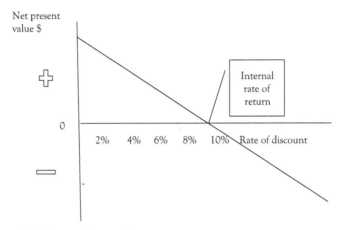

Figure 7.4 Internal rate of return

shown in Figure 7.4. This can be useful as organizations may set a high hurdle rate of return, which projects must achieve before they are accepted. Managers therefore readily understand that if a hurdle rate of 15 percent is to be achieved the IRR must be above the target.

Accounting Rate of Return and Profitability Index

Other methods that could be used include accounting rate of return in which the profit that can be earned is compared to the initial investment, or an average investment, to create a measure based on profitability.

$$\frac{\text{Profit on investment}}{\text{Average investment}} \times 100 = \% \text{ return}$$

A profitability index can be created, which compares different projects based on a calculation of the value per unit of investment.

$$\frac{\text{Present value of future cash flows}}{\text{Initial investment}} = \text{Profitability index}$$

Real Options

An approach that is becoming more popular is known as real option analysis. This recognizes that organizations often have multiple options available related to a strategic decision and, rather like financial market options, they create a right, rather than an obligation, to take action. For example, with respect to the Bangladesh project there are several options. Management could delay the project, or adopt a graduated phased approach, for example, begin by exporting, then later establishing a local sales office, followed by establishing local production facilities, and finally setting up a local subsidiary company, or; abandon at any stage, or entirely. Using this approach makes management aware of the financial implications of implementing the various options that can be taken into account in the decision-making process.

Whatever method is used the accountant can undertake sensitivity analysis to understand the potential impact of inaccurate estimates, that is, what degree of error could be accommodated before the project becomes nonviable in financial terms. Long-term projects inevitably entail making estimates, which could prove to be incorrect due to environmental events beyond the control of the organization. Therefore testing the estimates can be a valuable exercise.

Investment appraisals are useful in a variety of strategic decisions, such as product development, market development, mergers and acquisitions, customer lifetime profitability, investment in assets such as new technologies, and when making any business case.

Risk Management

As noted earlier there is now an increased awareness of the need to consider strategic risk and the management of risk when making strategic decisions. Therefore, due to the increasing accountability and responsibility attached to good stewardship of organizations, in which accountants play a key role, this section briefly reviews the management of risk.

Toward a Definition of Risk

Risk is often seen as negative however, in business (and in investment), there is a risk-reward relationship, that is, the greater the risk, the greater the reward. Therefore not all risk is necessarily a bad thing. Luhmann (1996, p. 3) defines risk as "the threat or probability that an action or event will adversely or beneficially affect an organization's ability to achieve its objectives." This definition suggests that risk can be beneficial as well as adverse. The purpose of risk management is not to eliminate risk, as this might be too costly, but to manage the risk to an acceptable level—acceptable to whom?—the stakeholders, and almost certainly the key players.

Types of Risk

There are many different classifications or types of risk that organizations face. It is not the intention to provide a comprehensive list but typical headings might include:

- Business or operational—relating to the activities carried out within an organization.
- Financial—relating to the financial operation of a business.
- Environmental—relating to changes in the political, economic, social, and financial environment.
- International—economic and political.
- Reputation risk—caused by failing to address some other risk.

The Risk Management Process

There are some key steps in managing the risk—most of which are self-explanatory.

For example, the risk management process at Lego® sets out to manage the risk by identifying the risk early, ahead of the strategic decision, that is, they are taking the decision knowing what the risks are and how they could be mitigated. They then measure the risk on a risk impact scale. Based on previous experience they are able to assess the level of risk that a strategic decision poses to the organization and other stakeholders. This highlights the importance of monitoring decisions and their outcomes so that it contributes to organizational learning and can inform future decision making. Lego® also makes an assessment of the financial impact of the risk. A strategy is then developed to manage the risk, which includes delegating responsibility to managers.

The Committee of Sponsoring Organizations (COSO 2004) published guidelines on enterprise risk, which recognizes that risk occurs at all levels in the organization, for example, strategic, business, and operational, as well as in all functions. It is also worth noting that many corporate governance codes of practice and laws that have been implemented in different countries require organizations to identify the risks associated with the business and how they intend to manage them.

A typical risk management process is set out in Figure 7.5.

A key point to note is that risk is the responsibility of the board of directors; however, they can delegate to a risk management group within the organization, often with a risk manager in charge, but it remains the board's overall responsibility. The starting point is the business strategy as this will ensure that the specific risks associated with a certain course of action are identified. When evaluating risks the risk appetite is an important concept as individuals have different appetites. For example, some individuals are risk averse, while others are risk loving, and others are risk neutral. The board of directors will include a mix of individuals, all with individual risk appetites, but collectively, via their strategic decisions, the board will exhibit a risk appetite of its own. This is significant as the risk appetite of a board will impact and send a signal on their

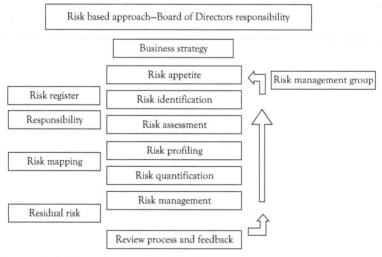

Figure 7.5 The risk management process

willingness to accept and manage risk, which will attract certain types of investors.

The risk identification stage is self-explanatory in that the risks are identified and most importantly are then logged in a risk register with the responsibility being assigned to an individual. This ensures that someone actually takes responsibility for managing the risk.

The stages of risk assessment, profiling, and quantification merge together in that they involve identifying the type of risk, determining the degree of risk, and estimating the potential impact (including the financial impact) of the risk.

The ultimate objective is to manage risk to an acceptable level as it is not always possible to eliminate risk altogether. However, the organization must assess whether the residual risk is acceptable to the key stakeholders. The final element is to review the risk and risk management strategy on a regular basis, particularly in light of the changing business environment. For example, the growing incidence of cybercrime creates additional risks for organizations that can have reputational impacts.

Management Accounting in Support of Strategic Evaluation

Impact on Stakeholder Groups

The explanation of stakeholder analysis illustrates that evaluating strategic decisions is much wider than just the financial analysis. Accountants can assist the analysis by evaluating the possible impact of stakeholder actions on a particular strategy by carrying out sensitivity or scenario analysis taking into account different outcomes—in short, to evaluate the financial impact of stakeholder actions.

Investment Appraisal and Business Case

Providing assistance in terms of undertaking investment appraisal techniques to evaluate the financial viability of strategic options, and assisting in the development of a business case to persuade, inform, and educate stakeholders where necessary.

Closure of the Gap

Following on from the investment appraisal and business case the accountant is able to quantify the extent to which the strategies will close the profits gap.

Evaluation of Risk and Monitoring

Evaluating the financial risks of strategic options and the costs of risk management measures and assisting in the implementing and monitoring of appropriate controls.

CHAPTER 8

Implementation Issues

Management Accounting in Support of Strategic Implementation

It could be said that the most difficult part of the strategic management process is the implementation phase. The accountant is well placed to aid with this aspect as the strategic plan needs communicating and, the first year at least, needs crystallizing into an operational plan.

Crystallizing the Strategic Plan into an Operational Budget

Once the strategic plan is agreed the key to implementation is ensuring that the plan is communicated effectively throughout the organization. The use of operational budgets is a common approach that is utilized to control activities and is often seen as an annual exercise. However, the practice of using budgets as a means of articulating the long-term plan in financial terms can be a good way of demonstrating the strategic intent. Plans can be expressed in financial terms with the early years being shown in more detail than future years. For example, the first year is expressed as a detailed operational budget, but the second year is expressed in quarterly targets with the third and subsequent years being represented as annual headline targets. This can be operated in the form of rolling budgets which are updated every quarter. At the end of each quarter the plan is extended so that the next 12 months is always shown in detail. This can keep the strategic plan alive, under constant review, and flexible enough to allow for change if the organization needs to respond to environmental or indeed internal factors.

This has implications for how the annual budget is developed. It should be an articulation of the strategic plan and not just an incremental budget based on the previous year. The plan should incorporate the strategic initiatives that have been formulated to close any gap that emerged from the corporate appraisal or SWOT analysis. This will take into account any changes in the environment and incorporate any resource requirements to achieve the strategic objectives. Budgets are often done in isolation to the strategic plan and prepared by the departmental/functional managers and therefore do not derive from the strategic analysis. The strategic objectives need to be communicated to the business units in terms of agreed targets so that managers can develop their budgets based on achieving the strategic objectives.

Budgetary Control with Latest Estimated Forecast or Trend

Once developed and agreed the monitoring of budgets needs to include the reporting of a trend or estimated forecast. This can be achieved by reporting the actual period results against budget/plan, together with the year to date and the future estimated forecast, as illustrated in the headings shown in Table 8.1.

The idea behind the representation in Table 8.1 is that the latest estimated forecast of the total year allows business units to express what they think they will be able to achieve, given the changes in the environment and resource position, since the original plan was developed. The reporting of the current year ties into the need to produce financial accounts for publication and communication to shareholders. This not only provides an early warning of any potential gap but also indicates that business unit managers need to be aware of their business environment and the progress toward achieving strategic objectives. The use of rolling budgets on a

Table 8.1 Typical headings for reporting actual results with latest estimated forecast

Description Income and expense headings	This period		Year to date		Total year	
	Actual	Plan	Actual	Plan	Latest estimated forecast	Plan

quarterly basis can also assist in this process, as the process of forecasting becomes part of the normal job. However, there is a danger that managers fall into the trap of simply extending the actual to-date and extrapolating a trend line to indicate the future, when the ideal is that managers proactively manage the future, not merely extend current trends. This is a key area where the accountant is able to contribute to ensure that the budgeting, reporting, and forecasting activities support the strategic management process.

Tailoring the Accounting System to the Strategy and Using Appropriate Reporting

The accounting system needs to be tailored to support the overall strategy. For example, Ward (1992) identified that the focus of the accounting techniques employed by organizations adopting a cost leadership strategy would be different to those utilized by an organization adopting a strategy of differentiation. In this way the accounting system supports the implementation of strategy. If the strategy changes the accounting focus will need to change.

The reporting structure can also support the strategic management process by focusing reporting on the future. Many management reports spend 80 percent of the report explaining the difference between the actual and the plan, whereas the focus should really be on the implications for the future and what can be done to ensure the achievement of objectives.

Ward (1992) makes a distinction between engineered and discretionary costs.

Engineered costs demonstrate a direct relationship between inputs and outputs. For example, a vehicle assembly plant takes component parts and assembles them into a complete vehicle with a given specification. The most important aspect to control is to ensure that the process is undertaken as efficiently and effectively as possible, to a given quality standard. The main emphasis is on productivity and efficiency measures of performance. Accounting techniques such as ABC can highlight areas where management needs to focus attention to improve the performance. ABC is not just a technique for costing products, but can be utilized to highlight areas where there is scope to reduce the cost of certain activities in order to support the cost leadership strategy. It is not the technique itself but the way the output of the technique is utilized to support strategy implementation that is important. Similarly if utilized within target costing ABC can help to identify areas where costs can be reduced in order to achieve a competitive advantage on new products. Developing a good understanding of costs over a period of time through the detailed analysis of everyday operations can be fed into developing operational strategies that support the overall strategic objective, that is, based on the experience curve how will costs reduce as the product gains a market share of 20 percent? This can be fed into the pricing strategy of new products, or entering new markets. Linked to the portfolio analysis this can help to establish the level of investment required, which might include initial losses on the product, to gain a strong market share.

ABC, however, will not necessarily help to the same extent with the marketing budget to launch the new product. Marketing is a discretionary cost and therefore an appropriate technique needs to be used when setting and reporting the marketing costs. An appropriate technique would be an objective-based approach where the budget is based on the marketing activity required to achieve the objective. This again can be based on experience and knowledge of the likely competitive responses. The reporting of costs against the achievement of objectives can be helpful in building up the required experience of how effective different marketing activities are in building or maintaining market share, even though there may be no direct relationship.

Responsibility Accounting

The use of responsibility accounting can aid implementation and subsequent monitoring in that the reporting of income and costs follows the responsibility of the managers. The separation of controllable and noncontrollable costs can be useful in motivating managers to use the report proactively. For example, if managers are judged based on a figure including centrally allocated costs, valuable time and resources can be wasted arguing about the validity of the bases used to allocate the costs. Striking a controllable costs/profit line can focus managers' attention on improving the performance of their area of responsibility toward meeting strategic objectives.

If, however, the allocated costs are also shown after the controllable subtotal, it highlights to managers that there are costs incurred that are the responsibility of others that support their business unit/function. This can encourage business unit managers to challenge the basis of allocation and the level of costs incurred, without becoming too emotive, while also ensuring that managers responsible for organizationwide costs, such as central marketing, and management support including accounting, are held accountable by those they serve, as well as those to whom they report. The concept of internal suppliers and customers is a useful way of thinking about the relationship between operational and central service functions. This can ensure that the central services provided are appropriate to the needs of the business units.

Ensuring That the Systems Are Developed to the Changing Needs of the Business

Accounting systems are often notorious for becoming legacy systems within an organization as the system that was purchased 10 years ago is no longer able to cope with the demands placed on it by the current business. All systems develop entropy over time and it is important to ensure that the systems are able to develop as the business develops. In this respect it is suggested by IT specialists that the system should be an open system capable of being developed as the organization's information needs change. Accounting systems have improved considerably over the years to an extent that much of the information required by managers is available to access via their desktop terminals, computers, and personal computing devices, often remotely from the office. This can be an advantage as the role of the accountant is no longer just to provide the numbers, but to aid interpretation and support decision making at all levels. However, financial information in the hands of nonfinancial managers can sometimes be the cause of incorrect decision making, therefore the accountant needs to adopt a supportive role and often that of an educator and mentor in the use of the financial information.

Business Partnering

There is often a need for accountants to support managers by the provision of training in the use of the reports provided by the system or the accountant. This is an aspect of business partnering, which is being actively promoted by the professional accounting bodies, accounting firms, and consultants. The role of the management accountant is much more about getting involved with the business and working with the business managers. Management accountants now need a good understanding of how the business works and how organizations formulate strategies in order that they can assist in the process.

There are several elements that need to be present in order for the accountant to become involved in the strategic management process. These are shown in Figure 8.1 and can be grouped under the three headings of accountant-led factors, organizational-led factors, and practical factors.

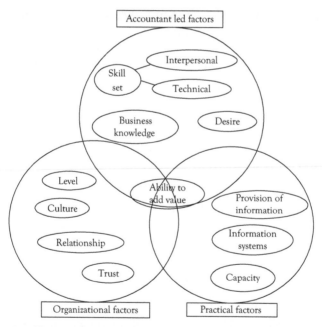

Figure 8.1 Factors determining the ability of accountants to be involved in the strategic management process (Pitcher 2015*)

* The support of the Chartered Institute of Management Accountants' General Charitable Trust is gratefully acknowledged in funding this research.

The accountant-led factors include the skill set of the accountant. It is not just the technical skills that are required but more importantly the soft skills—communications, team working, ability to persuade and influence, and so on—that are required. A good understanding of how a business works and a high degree of commercial acumen are desirable as well as a desire to become involved in the process. It is often easy for the accountant working in industry or the commercial world to sit in the office in front of the computer screen producing spreadsheets, but the real value added is when the accountant is away from the desk working with managers. This leads into the organizational factors in that the structure and culture of the organization can assist the accountant in being able to build relationships with the business unit and functional managers. This is influenced by the level at which the accountant works within the organization and the level at which strategy is set, which is part of the culture. However, if the accountant is in a position to access managers and build a relationship it requires trust. This is built up over a period of time. As the accountant begins to work more closely with managers the managers begin to trust the accountant's input and therefore actively seek out the help of the accountant. Thus the accountant becomes more involved in the strategic management process.

A significant factor can be the practicalities, such as how much time the accountant has available to become involved. If the resources available to the accountant are such that most of the time is spent in gathering the information required for monitoring and reporting, there is often very little time left to become involved in the strategic management process. This emphasizes the importance of ensuring that the accounting system is adequate for the business needs. The easier it is to produce the numbers the more time can be spent on analysis, interpretation, and determining the potential future implications.

CHAPTER 9

Multidimensional Performance Management

Traditional Performance Measurement

Traditional performance measurement systems tended to focus on financial performance measurement, particularly measures of profitability and capital efficiency. The reporting focus is based on historical information that may indicate a problem, but does little to help fix it or highlight the potential impact on future performance. By the time the measure is reported it could be too late. The measure often ignores what lies behind the financial measurement such as innovation, customer satisfaction, employee morale, the effectiveness of business processes, and where value is added or destroyed.

A Multidimensional Approach to Performance Management

A framework known as the balanced scorecard was developed by Kaplan and Norton (1996) that enables organizations to think about performance monitoring from a number of different perspectives other than just financial. The organization's vision and mission are the heart of the framework and thus all performance measures stem from what the organization is seeking to do in business terms. It provides a means to translate the vision and mission into a set of performance measures that facilitate the implementation of the organization's strategy. The interlinkages between performance measures can also be highlighted, which aids the understanding of the implications of new or revised strategies.

The primary framework suggested includes viewing the organization from four main perspectives.

- Customer perspective (how do customers see us?)
- Internal business process perspective (what must we excel at?)
- Learning and growth perspective (how to improve and create value? How will we ensure that we are in business in the future?)
- Financial perspective (how do we look to our shareholders?)

Organizations are encouraged to design perspectives that suit their particular organization and should not feel restricted to the four aforenoted perspectives. For example, a supermarket may consider performance measures in the form of financial, customers, suppliers, operations (business processes), community, and learning and growth. The main focus is to create a scorecard that monitors perspectives that are seen as important to the achievement of strategy, and that includes financial and nonfinancial, internal and external focus, quantitative and qualitative, and short-term and long-term measures. The use of lagging (backward looking) and leading (forward looking) performance measures is also encouraged. Other authors, such as Atkinson, Waterhouse, and Wells (1997), suggest that a stakeholder approach can be taken. If an organization takes into account the stakeholders in making strategic decisions, and each stakeholder has different expectations, it follows that different measures of performance will need to be utilized to know that an organization is meeting these expectations, as each stakeholder will judge the success of the organization by different criteria.

Kaplan and Norton suggest that four elements can be considered under the various perspectives adopted.

- Objective or goal
- Measure
- Target
- Initiative

The objective should be derived from the organization's strategy. The measure is derived from the objectives and should provide the answer to the question, what needs to be measured in order to know whether the objective has been met? This is sometimes overcomplicated when in practical terms using the simplest measure is the most appropriate. This has implications for the information systems. The information needs to be available in order to measure the degree to which the objectives have been achieved. Creating a complex form of measurement increases the costs associated with data collection and can result in managers not really understanding how the performance can be improved. The measure needs to aid the understanding of whether the strategy is working.

As a simple example, suppose an objective is to increase sales revenue. This can be measured by comparing sales revenue last year with sales revenue this year. This does not, however, indicate why this has happened. It could simply be as a result of price increases. But suppose the intention was to achieve this by increasing the customer base to attract and retain a higher number of customers. A nonfinancial measure of comparing the number of customers last year with the number of customers this year helps to determine this. However, increasing the number of customers does not necessarily mean that sales revenue will increase, as the sales revenue is also influenced by the volume of purchases made by each customer, so this could be linked to an objective to increase the average spend by individual customers over that achieved last year. Sales revenue is also linked to customer satisfaction levels (a qualitative objective) and customer retention rates. The qualitative objectives also need to be quantified, for example, to increase the customer satisfaction so that 95 percent of customers are happy this year.

The design process can be a valuable tool in gaining a thorough understanding of how the business actually works and actions that impact on more than one perspective. Kaplan and Norton were keen to stress that measures should link together and that the use of redundant measures that do not help the organization achieve its objectives should be avoided. It is therefore important to understand the interlinkages between objectives and measures.

For example, suppose a supermarket has a number of checkouts that can be opened to service customers. During quiet periods the supermarket does not want staff members occupying checkouts that are not being utilized and conversely, in busy periods, a buildup of queuing customers is undesirable. Therefore an objective may be to achieve optimum utilization of checkouts. This could be monitored by average queuing time

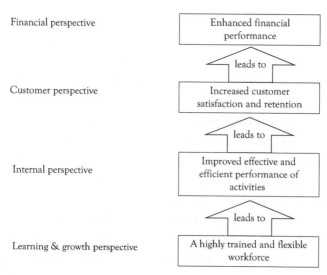

Financial perspective — Enhanced financial performance

Customer perspective — Increased customer satisfaction and retention

Internal perspective — Improved effective and efficient performance of activities

Learning & growth perspective — A highly trained and flexible workforce

Figure 9.1 Linkages between scorecard perspectives

at various times during the day, and the utilization of checkouts. This impacts on customer satisfaction levels and possibly customer retention, as well as utilization of staff. It has implications for the customer perspective and the business processes as well as staff training and employee morale. Hence there is a need to understand the interlinkages between the different perspectives as shown in Figure 9.1.

Targets can be utilized as a means of improving performance year on year and can form part of a performance management system at an individual level. Everyone in an organization has objectives, for which targets can be established.

The initiative provides the opportunity for the organization to ask, is there anything that can be done differently to aid the achievement of the objectives? This means that the balanced scorecard can be used as a developmental tool. It stops performance targets being rolled over each year without challenging the status quo.

Example of a Balanced Scorecard

The following example indicates that the balanced scorecard should relate directly to the strategy of the organization. All too often organizations continue to monitor the same performance elements each year without taking account of the changes in strategy.

HW Inc. Retail Stores

HW Inc. operates in the homeware market with retail stores in major cities around the world. The stores and online offering includes electrical goods, clothing, and home and garden products. The retail stores are mostly high-street stores although HW Inc. is planning on opening an out-of-town store in China where it has already been relatively successful with a small store in a "shopping village." A shopping village is an out-of-town location where retailers have small outlets that are often devoted to selling end-of-season goods and disposing of surplus inventories. These are normally sold at a discounted rate to the latest products available in their high-street stores.

The retail stores have not been as profitable in recent years as the market has become very competitive and customers are becoming more sophisticated and demanding in their expectations. One way in which HW Inc. has attempted to compete is to always offer the latest products. This makes inventory obsolescence an issue as judging the amount of inventory to hold so as to satisfy customer demand without having large inventory write-offs can be difficult. This is a problem in the clothing market where products are seasonal, for example, summer range, winter range, and so on. This sector is also one heavily influenced by the latest fashions. However, a new inventory management system is helping with the problem. The growth of the "click and collect" service is working well along with online sales, both of which are set to grow in the future.

The use of concessions (companies that effectively rent space in the HW Inc. stores) is also a method of providing a wide range of products to their customers and HW Inc. plans to try and increase the number of concessions in the next few years as it shares some of the risks between the partner companies. However, HW Inc. does not want to diminish the HW Brand and also plans to continue to develop and sell its own brand products. They also wish to retain their manufacturing capability as this provides a useful diversification from retailing and enables more control over quality of the home and garden product lines in which they have a manufacturing capability.

Clothing sales have been slowing in recent years but the furniture sales are fairly strong. The electrical goods market is very competitive particularly the audio-visual and kitchen aids ranges. The increased competition in the specialist electrical goods retailers has also hit the departmental stores such as HW along with the need to always be seen to stock the latest products.

Table 9.1 illustrates a range of performance measures that could be used to aid the achievement of this strategy. Appropriate targets would be set, but note how the performance measures have been kept relatively simple and relate directly to the objective.

Table 9.1 Balanced scorecard for HW Inc. retail stores

Objective	Measure	Initiative
Retail stores		
Financial perspective To increase sales per square foot	Difference in sales per square foot in year compared to previous year	Hire specialist consulting firm to review store layout to facilitate flow of customers and display of products to enhance sales volumes.
To increase average profit per retail outlet	Difference in average profit/(loss) of retail outlets in year compared to previous year	
Customer perspective Increase the footfall and conversion rate for in-store purchases	Difference in footfall and conversion rate this year compared to previous year	Hire specialist to review advertising, particularly window displays to attract customers. Link to previously mentioned store layout review.
Increase repeat customers	Number of repeat use of store card or credit card number this year compared to previous year	Marketing of store card coupled with more targeted mailshot marketing including tailored offers to existing customers where address is known
Increase customer satisfaction score	Customer satisfaction score based on survey	Undertake customer survey or install polling points at checkouts in stores
Internal business perspective Reduce average inventory holding time	Difference in inventory turnover this year compared to previous year	Ensure all staff are trained in the new inventory management system to enhance understanding of report outputs from the system and actions to take

To increase the use of concessions in store	Number of concession operators this year compared to previous year	Encourage concessions in store by offering incentives to operators during the first year of operation
Learning and growth perspective To develop and launch five new product ranges in household furniture (to build on strong market position)	Number of new products launched in year that achieved breakeven sales volume	Conduct marketing research to identify customer preferences in household furniture
To open stores in out-of-town shopping villages in three countries	Number of new stores in shopping villages opened during the year and in which countries	Undertake marketing research to identify suitable countries for shopping village outlets

Critical Success Factors and Interlocking Scorecards

Another concept that is important in performance measurement is identifying the critical success factors. A critical success factor is addressing the question, what does the organization need to be good at in order to achieve its objectives? The next logical question is, how does the organization know that it is good at what it needs to be good at? This helps to determine the key performance indicator that in turn helps to drive the information needs, that is, understanding the information required in order to monitor the achievement of strategy. This process also ensures that the right aspects of the business are being measured, and can stop information overload.

Developing the concept of critical success factors means that the senior management of an organization do not need to monitor every single performance measure, but can focus on the critical success factors. This is because they delegate responsibility to lower levels of the organization for more detailed aspects of the business operations. These tiered levels of management can have their own balanced scorecard so, instead of one organizational scorecard that would be difficult to manage, a series of nested scorecards can be created and monitored at different levels of responsibility. The key is ensuring that employees at all levels are aware of how their individual role fits into the overall scheme of things. It is suggested that the balanced scorecard, and resultant strategy map indicating the linkages between the perspectives, can be used as a communication tool to ensure employees at all levels understand the organization's strategy and their role in its achievement.

There can be some difficulties with the balanced scorecard in that establishing too many measures can confuse managers and the strategic focus can be lost. The behavioral implications of introducing a balanced scorecard also need to be taken into account as employees can become concerned when performance is being monitored closely. However, the process of introducing the approach should be inclusive and, if done with the involvement at all levels, can be very positive in that all employees understand the organization's strategy.

Performance Management in Service Organizations

An approach for performance measurement in service sector organizations was put forward by Fitzgerald et al. (1991) and highlights that the traditional approach of monitoring only the financial perspective is in danger of focusing on the results and ignoring the determinants. The multidimensional approach to avoid this is shown in Figure 9.2.

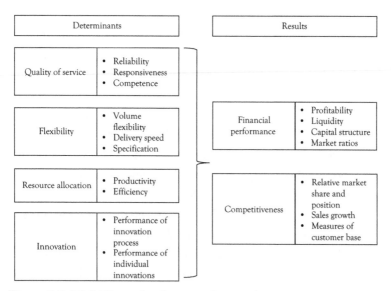

Figure 9.2 Multidimensional approach to performance management for service organizations

The secret to performance measurement is to gain an understanding of what determines success. This can be built up over a period of time via the use of a range of multidimensional measures. Performance measurement, however, is only part of the wider concept of performance management. Therefore for the measurement to mean anything the results have to inform management such that it stimulates appropriate actions.

Simons' Levers of Control

Simons' (1994) levers of control are often utilized as a framework for categorizing the type of controls that an organization can use. In practice an organization will utilize a range of controls, but due to its culture it might use a predominance of one of these, for example, a highly controlled bureaucratic organization might use a predominance of diagnostic controls, whereas a meritocracy and organization that gives employees more autonomy might use a predominance of interactive and belief controls. Therefore the culture of the organization, as well as the strategy, has an impact on the type of controls that would be adopted. This implies that the design of management accounting systems can help to support and develop the culture of the organization.

- Diagnostic use of control systems—ex post monitoring, corrective action, and management by expectations.
- Interactive use of control systems—frequent use and dialog to stimulate organizational learning and change.
- Belief systems—communication of core values related to sustainability to trigger change in mindsets and support organizational change processes (e.g., mission statements).
- Boundary systems—restraining organizational members from entering in an extreme zone (e.g., code of conducts, anti-bribery guidelines).

Divisional Performance

When an organization is structured in a way that has divisions or subsidiaries, it is useful to be able to set targets and monitor the performance of each division separately and, if sensible, to make comparisons. When comparing divisional performance it is important to make sure that the comparison is meaningful and that other factors are taken into account. For example, two divisions undertaking the same activity, but operating in different countries, may perform differently, due to the economic conditions prevailing in their market, such as the U.S. economy performing differently to Asian economies. Therefore differences in performance are not just due to management performance. This emphasizes the importance of monitoring external environmental PESTEL factors and how they impact on different markets and the significance of comparing performance against competitors in the same market.

Levels of Performance Monitoring of Business Units

Organizations can be divided into strategic business units or operating/ functional units for the purposes of monitoring performance. Typically functional units are treated as cost centers in which costs are allocated to the functional units, and monitored against a cost budget. If the organization is able to identify business units to which revenue streams and costs can be meaningfully allocated, they can be treated as profit centers. In this case a series of profitability ratios could be utilized as financial performance indicators, for example, operating profit percentage. In cases where it is possible to allocate capital items, such as plant and equipment, buildings, and so on, the business units can be monitored as investment centers. Suitable financial performance indicators in this case might be return on investment.

In all cases costs, revenues, and capital items need to be allocated on a meaningful basis, otherwise the monitoring is not helpful. It is also important to be able to monitor and report those costs that are controllable by the manager responsible for the business unit or cost unit. Apportioning costs such as central marketing costs can create time-consuming discussions and wasted resources if managers feel they are being penalized for something outside of their control. The preferred approach is to strike a line at controllable profit, or cost, and then show apportioned costs separately below the controllable line. This enables the managers to take ownership of their area of responsibility, but keeps in front of them the fact that the unit benefits from decisions that are made centrally, and that there is in fact a cost attached to those activities to which they are expected to contribute. This becomes more relevant when central service costs are allocated to business units.

For example, consider the use of a central IT function in organizations. If a central IT function is treated as a cost center and costs are not charged out to users, it can encourage users to request more and more services, as there is no cost to the user. However, if charges are made to divisions at cost of provision, based on usage, business units are aware that IT services cost money and are more prudent and careful in their requests. They may well undertake a cost–benefit analysis before requesting additional IT services. Indeed the head office may well require a business case to be made before any additional investment is made. A further step could be made and the IT function makes a charge to divisions based on a market rate. This allows the IT function to operate as a business unit in its own right, which can result in IT staff being keen to "sell" services to divisions and actively seek out areas where they can provide assistance. Therefore, there is a motivational aspect for the IT function derived from the approach taken to charging internal services.

One way of establishing a market rate is to investigate what it would cost the organization to outsource its IT function. By investigating this it sets an external benchmark against which the IT function can be measured, and in some instances it may be more cost—efficient to outsource some of the basic IT functions. There are, however, strategic aspects here such as loss of control, confidentiality, and so on that need to be taken into account, again illustrating that cost is not the only consideration. This idea can take an extra dimension in that large organizations may decide that divisions can buy certain IT services from external providers, that is, they do not have to use the central IT function. This can add a degree of competitiveness to the IT function in that it encourages efficiency and effectiveness within the in-house function. A possibility is that a function such as IT provision lends itself to a hybrid style of cost allocation. The provision of an organizationwide network is a decision that benefits the whole organization and is treated as a central "head office" cost. The costs of IT that are directly attributable to a business unit can be charged at cost to the units, for example, computers utilized by the business units become their assets, with the subsequent depreciation charges and so on. Additional bespoke services required by divisions are charged at a market rate. The design of such a cost allocation system can ensure that a service function such as IT is contributing to the overall strategy of the organization.

Return on Investment (ROI) and Residual Income (RI)

Two common methods of monitoring divisional performance are return on investment and residual income.

The return on investment is typically calculated as:

$$\frac{\text{Divisional profit before interest and tax (operating profit)}}{\text{Investment in the division}} \times 100 = \%$$

ROI is frequently utilized to compare divisional performance. However, it is important to compare performance against external benchmarks if available.

For example, economic performance is as much an issue as is managerial performance. If a division in Hong Kong is making 25 percent ROI, yet the division in the United States is making a loss of 3 percent, does it mean that the management team of the division in Hong Kong is better? Apart from the fact that divisions may be operating in different sectors, competitor organizations in Hong Kong may be making 30 percent, in which case the Hong Kong division is not doing as well as it should. Or if the competition in the United States is losing 5 percent, then the U.S. division is actually doing quite well.

This underlines the fact that external information, particularly of competitors, needs to be taken into account when making judgments about the managerial performance of divisions. This also highlights the need to set targets with external reference points rather than taking a purely internal viewpoint.

The residual income is typically calculated as shown in Table 9.2.

Table 9.2 Calculation of residual income

	$
Divisional profit before interest and tax (operating profit)	x
Less a charge for the use of capital (notional interest)	(x)
Residual income	X

One aspect to note is that residual income is normally expressed as an absolute figure and is positive or negative. This is useful as a performance measure when the investment in the division is primarily controlled by the head office. In some instances this is said to be a better measure to use when considering further investments as it can reduce some of the behavioral implications of the ROI measure.

Suppose a division has achieved a ROI of 20 percent, beating the target set by head office of 15 percent. The management team, who are keen to demonstrate continued high performance, may be reluctant to undertake a project that yields 17.5 percent. Although it is above the head office target, if the division undertakes the project it will reduce its average ROI to below 20 percent, and make the division look as if its performance has declined. Therefore there is a dysfunctional or motivational aspect to ROI. As RI is an absolute figure, if the project increases the RI by $100,000 then, all other things being equal, the management would be more motivated to undertake the project. RI utilizes the concept of net present value discussed in Chapter 7 and is said to have the same properties in decision making, that is, a positive outcome encourages acceptance, whereas a negative outcome discourages acceptance.

Economic Value Added

Economic value added (EVA™) was developed by a firm of consultants (Stern Stewart & Co., now Stern Value Management) as a means of measuring company performance. The economic value is the net operating profit after tax from which a deduction is made for the use of capital in the form of a capital charge, based on the weighted average of cost of capital, to arrive at the economic value, shown in Table 9.3.

It is an absolute value, that is, a number rather than a percentage, and in a similar way to RI, if used as an investment appraisal method,

Table 9.3 *Calculation of economic value added*

	$
Adjusted profits to arrive at net operating profits after tax	x
Capital charge (adjusted capital employed x weighted average cost of capital)	(x)
Economic value added	x

would encourage managers to undertake an investment if it increased the economic value added. In this way it is said to be a good measure as it encourages managers to make decisions based on the interests of the shareholders and the organization as a whole.

Stern Stewart recommended that adjustments should be made to the financial accounting profit to derive an adjusted net operation profit. The typical adjustments include adding back noncash items and accounting adjustments, such as depreciation. This is to arrive at a figure that is closer to cash generated. Other typical adjustments include research and development, marketing, and training. The basic justification for adjusting these items is that they are an investment in generating future revenue streams rather than a charge against profits in the year in which they are incurred. An adjustment is made to treat them as investments and therefore added to the balance sheet to be written off over the period for which they are deemed to be generating revenue and, hopefully, profits. For example a marketing campaign, particularly in the case of a new product, or indeed the research and new product development costs, may generate profits over a longer period than one year. Therefore it would seem logical that the associated costs should be written off over the same period of time to which they contribute to profits. EVA™ can be a difficult concept for nonfinance managers to understand the significance of the adjustments, therefore in practical terms adjustments are made if:

- It is likely to have a material impact on EVA™.
- Managers are able to influence the outcome.
- The operating people can readily understand it.
- The required information is relatively easy to track or derive.

Benefits and Drawbacks of EVA™

EVA™ is said to have several uses that may be of interest to an organization. For example, it can be used to set organizational goals and therefore could feature as a performance measure and target on a balanced scorecard. It can be used to determine bonuses at a divisional and whole organizational level and may be a way of motivating managers to increase economic value. It can also be used to value companies and determine equity investments, by focusing on the value added potential of the organization.

EVA™ also introduces an element of accountability to divisional managers for investment decisions that benefit the company in the long term. This approach encourages managers to think about the long-term issues rather than attempting a short-term fix. It also makes managers think along the lines of shareholders in terms of adding value to the business.

However, as with most techniques there are some issues that an organization needs to be aware of if thinking of using EVA™ as a performance measure. It is complex and managers who do not have a financial background can also find it difficult to understand and therefore there will be a requirement for training and support at all levels in the organization. As it is a single financial measure it is best utilized as part of a multidimensional approach to performance management.

There is also a high degree of subjectivity in estimating the length of time that items such as research and development, marketing, and training continue to generate revenue streams and, therefore, the period over which they should be written off.

Key Factors to Consider When Implementing EVA™

There are some key factors that can be considered when implementing EVA™ as a key driver for performance management.

- It is important to ensure that everyone in the organization understands the concept of economic value added and that there is an agreement on the definition of organizational success.
- The overall strategy may need reformulating to focus on adding value with a resultant review of strategic direction and priorities.
- The cost of capital needs to be calculated and in some instances this can be a useful exercise for an organization. Often organizations are not aware of their cost of capital and therefore no real view as to the level of profit required to satisfy the capital providers who may be considered a significant stakeholder in many decisions.

- The use of external benchmarks is encouraged, which can benefit the organization by providing the incentive to improve.
- It can be utilized as targets for key employees, and indeed all employees, in viewing how they can add value. It can also be linked to a reward system.
- Introducing EVA™ may well involve a cultural change to focus employees on thinking about value added, not just to shareholders but to stakeholders.
- There could be implications for the accounting system in that it will need to be adapted toward highlighting economic value added. It may in some instances require investment in information systems. In order to facilitate the use of EVA™ reporting it is important to avoid accounting complexity and keep it simple. There may also be a significant amount of training to undertake of managers to enable them to fully understand the concept.
- The value drivers need to be identified so that they become the focus of strategy and that the budgeting and strategic plans are fully integrated toward EVA™.

The Issue of Transfer Pricing in Divisional Performance

The rationale behind transfer pricing is to identify where value is added within the internal value system, to aid the monitoring of divisional performance, and to assist managers with decision making that maximizes the economic benefit for the organization as a whole. Setting transfer prices that encourage efficient internal trading can be a key part of implementing a successful strategy, and extracting the maximum value for the customer. It can have motivational implications for the managers of business units, particularly across international borders, and encourage goal congruency and the achievement of the overall strategy.

The need for transfer pricing typically occurs in situations where Division A manufactures a product that is utilized in a product or service

	$	$
Materials	X	
Labor	X	
Direct (marginal) cost		X
Add manufacturing overheads	X	
Full manufacturing cost		X
Add delivery costs	X	
Add sales & marketing costs	X	
Add administration costs	X	
Total cost		X
Profit margin		X
Sales price		X

Marginal cost	✛	Profit

Full manufacturing cost	✛	Profit

Total cost	✛	Profit

Sales price

Figure 9.3 Basic cost structure and transfer price options

offered by Division B. This can have an added dimension if there is an external market for the product manufactured by Division A.

For example, Division A produces an electric motor that it sells on the open market, but is also a component part of the vacuum cleaner manufactured by Division B. There are also alternative motors on the open market that could be used by Division B. What price would encourage Division A to sell to Division B and motivate Division B to buy from Division A? Transfer pricing can have a significant impact on divisional performance monitoring when there are transfers between divisions, which is why managers often challenge and wish to negotiate the transfer price.

Figure 9.3 indicates the basic cost structure and transfer price options for a product manufactured in Division A and transferred (sold) to Division B.

Options For Transfer Pricing

Marginal Cost

In this instance Division A recovers the direct (marginal) costs of manufacturing the product, but is left with the manufacturing overhead. Division B would be more than happy to buy motors from Division A at this price.

Marginal Cost Plus

It could be argued that it is not fair on Division A just to receive the marginal cost, and leave it bearing all of the fixed cost. Hence it could be decided to transfer the motors at marginal cost plus a percentage markup to provide an incentive and contribution toward the fixed cost. As long as this transfer price is less than the price of other motors available in the open market, Division B will be happy to buy from Division A.

Full Manufacturing Cost

Another method might be to transfer at full manufacturing cost. This enables Division A to recover the fixed costs of manufacturing. It is better to calculate the transfer price using a standard (or budgeted) cost as if actual costs are transferred it does not encourage efficiency in Division A, as transferring the motor at actual cost means any inefficiency is transferred to Division B.

Full Manufacturing Cost Plus

It is also possible to add a percentage markup to the full manufacturing cost. Again if this is less than the price of a competitor motor in the open market it will still be beneficial to keep the business within the company and motivate Division B to buy from Division A.

Full Market Price

Another method is the use of market price. If, however, Division B could buy a product at a lower price on the open market it might not be motivated to buy from Division A. Of course the head office could insist that Division B uses Division A's motor and not allow it to buy on the open market, but this may de-motivate Division B and create tension between divisions when ideally the divisions need to work together.

Adjusted Market Price

An argument could be made that if Division A sells to Division B it saves on the direct selling costs, that is, it is an easy sale and could save on distribution costs. The market price could be adjusted, that is, reduced, by the savings made on selling and distribution costs.

Negotiated Prices

An alternative might be to allow divisional managers to negotiate a price between themselves. This could, however, take time and be detrimental to the business if decisions are needed quickly, in which case a policy that determines the price according to a prescribed basis is more beneficial.

All of the aforementioned assume that Division A has spare capacity and can satisfy external customer demand and the requirement from Division B. However, as soon as Division A has limited capacity, and has a choice to make as to whether it sells to Division B or to an external customer, the decision process changes. This is because in the situation of limited capacity, if a motor is sold to Division B, then Division A loses the opportunity to sell to an external customer. This raises the issue of a lost opportunity to sell at full market price to an external customer.

Opportunity Cost

When Division A has spare capacity the opportunity cost of producing one extra unit is the marginal cost, as this is the only additional cost to Division A of producing the extra unit. When, however, there is no spare capacity, Division A loses the contribution it would earn from selling to an external customer, on top of the marginal costs incurred. Therefore the opportunity cost is the marginal cost plus the lost contribution. If Division A makes the transfer to Division B the organization as a whole loses the contribution from the external customer and therefore the preferred option is to sell externally. The only exception to this is where Division B can add more value to the motor as part of its product than Division A can generate in the open market for the motor on its own. The use of the opportunity cost enables the decision to be made based on the benefit to the organization as a whole.

Transfer Pricing Across International Borders

When transferring products or services across international borders other factors should also be taken into account such as:

Tax Regimes

Different tax regimes and the view of local tax authorities to cross-border transfers (e.g., on allowable costs to be transferred).

Ethical Considerations

The transfer price should be justifiable, and hence ethically calculated, and not just used to transfer profits between countries, although there may well be an element of tax management within the decision.

Competitiveness

Degree of competitiveness of overseas market, for example, the transfer price should not make the overseas unit uncompetitive by charging a high transfer price.

Motivation

The motivational aspect of transfer pricing linked to the previously mentioned point. Local managers should feel that the price is fair and not just calculated for the benefit of the company tax bill.

Customers

The view of customers in that some may feel the price is inflated by the organization for no real reason, other than to make profits in an overseas location, that is, consumers are becoming suspicious. Customers in some markets are skeptical of overseas organizations charging higher prices in different markets. The recent tax avoidance scandals have heightened consumer awareness of transfer pricing issues and therefore the likely response of consumers might need to be considered.

Local Suppliers

The degree to which there are local suppliers of products that could supply the same product at a lower cost. In this instance the differentiation and quality control aspects of the product could be a key factor in justifying a higher price than that available in the local market.

Currency Risk

The currency in which the transfer is made, that is, who bears the foreign exchange risk. If the receiving overseas division bears the risk this could make profits fluctuate for no controllable reason. The performance management of overseas locations needs to take account of the economic and managerial performance. For example, in some markets it may be that it is not management actions that are generating higher profits, but the economic conditions. Therefore external benchmarks need to be made with other companies in the same sector in the same overseas market.

Benchmarking

Benchmarking is a means of comparing the performance of an organization (or individual or subgroup) with another with the aim of learning and making improvements. Whether following a strategy of cost leadership or differentiation, making continuous improvements to reduce costs or enhance the elements of differentiation can contribute to the sustainability of the competitive strategy, and hence the strategic management process. It is important to note that it is not just a copying exercise, as the context in which the improvements are being implemented needs to be taken into account. For example, if the management of an organization were to benchmark performance against a competitor that was much larger, the competitor may enjoy economies of scale that the organization will not be able to match, so just copying the practices of others may not yield any benefit unless it is tailored to the organization's particular situation.

Uses and Benefits of Benchmarking

Benchmarking can also be utilized as a means of developing new initiatives that can be implemented as part of a balanced scorecard approach to performance management. Also in relation to competitors it can aid the determination of strengths and weaknesses as part of the corporate appraisal or SWOT analysis. Therefore the process and outputs of benchmarking exercises can be utilized in conjunction with other techniques to aid the development of strategy and the achievement of objectives.

One of the key advantages of benchmarking is that it can aid in setting aspirational targets that are linked to strategy, particularly if used as part of the initiatives within the balanced scorecard. This could be important for organizations that are experiencing poor performance and need to improve. It can also encourage innovation, something that is becoming more important for most industries in the future. It can also help to motivate employees via the use of targets but also because benchmarking involves all employees. It is not a process that is undertaken in isolation but should be inclusive and involve employees at all levels.

Difficulties of Benchmarking

There are, however, difficulties that organizations need to be aware of when undertaking benchmarking exercises. If targets are set and constantly missed it can have the opposite effect of motivating employees, but can demotivate them. Under certain forms of benchmarking, for example, competitor benchmarking, there is a danger of disclosing confidential or commercially sensitive information in an effort to gain some benefit from the exercise, that is, there may be a temptation to disclose too much information. The danger of just copying what others do is also a temptation without taking the time to assess how best to implement an improvement in the organization's particular context, that is, management become focused on the benchmark itself rather than learning from what they have found. Benchmarking also carries the assumption that suitable partners can be found with which to benchmark.

Classification of Benchmarking

There are many general classifications under which benchmarking is considered. These include internal and external, formal and informal, as well as others. However, the typical types of benchmarking that might be appropriate for any organization are as follows:

- Internal—comparing one operating unit or function with another in the same company, for example, one retail outlet against another, or one production unit against another. However, it is important to be aware that outlets in different parts of the country may be affected by different factors within their local context, although the operations may be the same.
- Functional/activity or best practice—internal functions are compared with the best external practitioners regardless of industry, for example, inventory control with a supermarket, or booking systems with a travel agent, hotel, theater, or airline.
- Competitor—with direct competitors, including reverse engineering techniques, that is, direct competitors, but we need to be careful that it is a meaningful comparison. Also this tends to be appropriate for aspects that can be benchmarked via publicly available data, for example, product ranges, prices, and so on.
- Strategic—aimed at strategic action and organizational change, for example, launching a new product, or product development. Even benchmarking against organizations that have successfully turned around a loss-making position to one of profitability could be a possibility for organizations that are performing poorly.
- Industry—there may be industry standards that can be utilized, for example, many industries have trade bodies that collect and anonymize data to produce industry benchmarks that could be used for comparison. The university sector is an industry about which there is much information provided by various bodies about universities and colleges that can be used for comparison.

Stages of a Benchmarking Exercise

There is no one definitive process for benchmarking but a typical series of stages that an organization could follow are outlined as follows:

1. Establish benchmarking objectives—it is important to have a clear idea of what it is that the management team wishes to achieve and what aspects of the business it is benchmarking.

2. Establish mixed-skills benchmarking team—benchmarking is inclusive and is not undertaken just by accountants. A team of people with a mix of skills and knowledge of the particular area is usually required. This also facilitates a sharing of knowledge and understanding within the company.

3. Develop relevant KPIs—it is important that the performance indicators are developed prior to collecting data as this determines what data is required. It is also important to recognize that the data has to be available from both parties if benchmarking with another organization.

4. Choose an organization or business unit against which to benchmark—choosing an appropriate benchmarking partner is important as the benchmark has to be meaningful and one from which the management team can learn. Also, if external, the partner will wish to learn from the exercise as well, that is, mutual benefit.

5. Measure own and partner's performance—the obvious stage of measuring performance of both parties on a comparable basis.

6. Analyze data and discuss results—once collected the data needs to be analyzed. It should also be recognized that the reason why there are differences in performance needs to be discussed as this may not always be apparent, that is, the management team need to understand the "why" behind the difference.

7. Implement change—any improvements that could be made need to be implemented, which brings into play change management issues as employees need to be included in the process.

8. Monitor improvements—the impact of changes needs to be monitored and often this is not immediately apparent as to why performance has or has not improved, particularly if a number of things have been changed as there may not be a direct link.

9. Publish success—an important step often overlooked is to publish the success of the exercise as this can act as a motivating factor for employees.

Behavioral Aspects of Performance Management

An aspect of performance management that we should not forget is that organizations are made up of people, and performance measurement may be subject to behavioral implications, or behavioral displacement. For example, there can be a tendency to depress bad news and focus on the positive aspects of performance, or manipulate performance measures to look good. Behavioral aspects occur in setting, measuring, and interpreting performance targets. For example, creating slack resources within the budget or setting soft targets needs to be guarded against. In situations where it becomes known that senior management will ask for the expense budget to be reduced there can be a tendency to inflate costs knowing that it will be reduced later. It is important, however, that the managers responsible are actively involved in the budget and target-setting process, in line with strategic objectives, as this will ensure their buy-in to the targets set.

Managers may undertake gaming activities, that is, focus on those areas they know are being monitored closely to the detriment of other areas. In some instances this can lead to suboptimal behavior as managers pursue a narrow range of objectives. Suboptimal behavior can occur in situations where managers' focus on local objectives, such as their own divisional return on investment target when it is detrimental to the organization as a whole.

Presenting a biased message can occur in reporting performance or interpreting results, where information is presented in a positive light by filtering out bad news, and focusing on the message the recipient wants to hear. Care has to be taken in choosing the performance measures as this can also create suboptimal behavior. For example, in health care focusing on reducing bed occupancy rates may encourage hospitals to send patients home earlier than normal, which reduces the days a patient occupies a bed. However, if the patient is readmitted later due to becoming ill again this is a new admittance and the bed occupancy starts from zero again, therefore the occupancy rates can remain artificially lower, but the patient recovery takes longer.

Behavioral aspects can emerge throughout the whole performance management process, hence their significance in the design and operation of management control systems. The best type of performance measure is one that is understood by all involved, is seen to be fair, and is equitable and can be monitored cost effectively. When performance is linked to reward systems it can present problems if seen to be unfair. When linking reward and pay there are several roles that the performance measurement system performs:

- Informational, that is, the performance measure used sends a signal to employees that management are focusing on a particular aspect of performance and employees will direct their efforts toward ensuring that performance is good.
- Motivational, that is, the particular measure used acts as a motivator for employees. However, note that performance requires more than just motivation, for example, it also requires the resources to do the job. This speaks for itself in that pay linked to performance is often intended as a motivator, but not all employees are motivated by money to the same extent and motivation is not the only element of good performance. For example, an employee may be highly motivated but if they don't have the resources to do the job then any amount of motivation won't help.
- Personnel-related, that is the performance measures used can attract certain types of employee to the organization. For example, if a sales force is paid a low salary but high performance bonus it will attract people who are confident of their own ability.
- Noncontrol purposes, for example, where pay is linked to organizational performance, perhaps via a "share-of-profits bonus scheme", the amount of the bonus, and hence the amount of cash required, will be less in poor performing years and can smooth remuneration payments to match the earnings of the organization.

The key to performance management systems is to match the objectives of employees with those of the organization. This will aid the implementation and achievement of strategy.

Management Accounting Support of Performance Management

Balanced Scorecard

Aiding the development of a balanced scorecard or multidimensional approach to performance measurement particularly in respect of crystallizing objectives into quantifiable performance measures.

Data Collection

Ensuring that the accounting systems are capable of collecting the data required to monitor performance in a meaningful and comparative format that is understood by managers.

Interpretation

Providing support in interpreting the performance measures and their implications for the achievement of strategy.

Evaluation

Assisting in the evaluation of divisional performance to ensure that divisions are motivated to achieve organizational performance and to avoid the incidence of dysfunctional behavior. This is significant in the establishment of transfer pricing regimes.

Benchmarking

Contributing to the process of benchmarking by providing financial input and expertise in performance measurement to benchmarking teams.

CHAPTER 10

Sustainability and Performance Management

Introduction

Sustainability is becoming increasingly significant for all organizations and a key aspect of strategy formulation and strategic choice, as well as a potential source of competitive advantage. It is therefore worth considering the contribution that accountants can make toward the achievement of an organization's sustainability objectives.

What Is Sustainable Development?

Two definitions help us understand what is meant by sustainable development and sustainability.

- Sustainable development is development that "meets the needs of the present without compromising the ability of future generations to meet their own needs" (United Nations World Commission on Environment and Development 1987).
- Sustainability refers to the "long-term maintenance of systems according to environmental, economic and social considerations" (Crane and Matten 2004).

Why Be Sustainable?

The cynical view might be that it is good public relations, but in some regulated industries it is a requirement and a legal obligation. There are also cost benefits to be gained, for example, from using energy more efficiently or reducing wastage, which provides a powerful business case for being sustainable.

The motivations for being sustainable can come from outside of the organization, such as regulatory bodies, governments, and public pressure groups. Professional accounting bodies are included among those promoting the reporting of sustainable practices and corporate governance codes are requiring an increasing amount of information to be published concerning sustainability issues. Issues such as the use of sustainable materials, recycling, and products made from recycled materials are actively being promoted by consumer groups. Governments in developed countries are prepared to legislate and levy taxes to discourage the use of materials and sale of products that are harmful to the environment. The need to be seen to be sustainable can be a significant influence on strategy development and strategy choices. Many organizations now produce an annual corporate social responsibility report demonstrating their commitment to sustainability, and include sustainability objectives within the strategic plan. Indeed in some instances it is the source of a competitive advantage or differentiating factor.

Reporting, Monitoring, and Control

The environmental standard ISO 14031 includes three types of performance indicators that provide a multidimensional platform for monitoring sustainability.

- Management performance indicators (MPIs)—policy, people, planning activities, practice, procedures, decisions, and actions in the organization;
- Operational performance indicators (OPIs)—inputs, the supply of inputs, the design, installation, operation and maintenance of the physical facilities and equipment, outputs, and their delivery;
- Environmental condition indicators (ECIs)—information about the local, regional, national, or global condition of the environment.

The balanced scorecard was discussed in Chapter 9 as a mechanism for considering performance from a range of perspectives. One aspect to consider is whether organizations should adopt a separate scorecard for sustainability or incorporate suitable measures within the overall organization's scorecard. A danger of keeping a separate scorecard is that sustainability becomes marginalized. Therefore incorporating measures into the organization's overall scorecard is said, by some authors, to be a preferable approach.

Management Accounting in Support of Sustainability

Corporate Social Responsibility (CSR) Report Input

Accountants are often involved in preparing the annual CSR report, which many organizations now produce in order to demonstrate and report on sustainable activities. This has increased the degree of accountability and transparency in managing and reporting organizational performance, which is an area in which accountants are always involved by way of the stewardship and governance roles within an organization.

Performance Management

The balanced scorecard approach to performance management can be a useful way of capturing aspects of sustainability. The accountant can play a key role in the development of suitable performance measures derived from the strategic objectives. The interpretation of performance measures and expressing the implications for the future in financial terms are key areas where accountants are able to contribute.

Monitoring Aspects of the Environment

The accountant will be monitoring the environment for economic indicators, interest rates, inflation, and so on that could impact on the organization's ability to achieve its strategic objectives. In doing so information might be identified concerning changes in industry standards or government policy that might require a more sustainable approach by industry members. In this way the accountant contributes to the data collection system feeding into the environmental analysis discussed in Chapter 2.

Development of Controls

An obvious area for accountants to contribute is in the development of controls, particularly the diagnostic controls. Also by encouraging the use of interactive controls, whereby employees are empowered to take control action for themselves can create a culture of learning within the organization. Benchmarking exercises also aid this perspective and the use of initiatives on the balanced scorecard, so that employees are encouraged to challenge the way things are done. Accountants can contribute to training programs by increasing the financial awareness of all employees and thus contribute to the development of staff, not just as an employee but also in broader terms to develop as a person, which contributes to social sustainability.

Cost Monitoring and Reporting

Specific costs can be monitored and reported, which benefits the company in achieving economic sustainability by enabling better management of costs. For example, energy costs, wastage, and cost of quality all contribute to environmental sustainability if systems are in place to facilitate their effective management.

Accounting and Management Techniques

The accountant is able to contribute expertise and knowledge of specific techniques that can be utilized to improve sustainability practices within the organization. Benchmarking exercises can be useful as a means of identifying the sustainable practice of other companies that could enhance an organization's own practice, and the accountant can be a useful member of a benchmarking project team. Life cycle costing can improve the sustainability of new product design and manufacture. The use of the value system analysis linked to ABC can aid the improvement of manufacturing processes by highlighting areas of inefficiency, which also increases the economic sustainability of the organization.

Cost-Benefit Analysis Within Investment Appraisal

Whenever organizations make strategic investment decisions accountants are in a good position to contribute to the evaluation by way of a cost-benefit analysis, including the tangible and intangible costs and benefits, which should also include the sustainability aspects of the decision.

Sustainable Profitability

The accountant is able to make a contribution to the overall sustainability of the organization through undertaking the normal role of helping to improve performance and inform decision making. Even contributing to halting the decline in profits of an ailing organization is contributing to economic sustainability. After all, if an organization is not profitable it won't be around long enough to contribute to the sustainability of the planet.

CHAPTER 11

The Future Role of the Management Accountant

The Continuing Need for Stewardship and Compliance

On January 15, 2018 Carillion plc, a British multinational facilities management and construction services company, went into liquidation. Carillion was the second largest construction company in the United Kingdom, employed 43,000 people around the world, and had subcontracts with as many as 30,000 small businesses. Following the financial difficulties during 2017 and three profit warnings, debts of £900 million, and a pension fund deficit estimated to be anywhere between £580 million and £1.4 billion, the banks finally decided enough was enough and refused to fund the business, forcing it into compulsory liquidation. This highlights the stewardship and compliance roles of the accountant, but also raises the issues of whether the management accounting was sufficient to enable managers to manage the business in a sustainable manner, or whether the managers took note of the management information provided. It is human nature to continue in the hope that things will get better, but denial is a state that management accountants should guard against. Part of the problem at Carillion was that many projects were of high risk and low margin. It is understandable in a competitive market that managers are prepared to take risks, but this should be done with the full knowledge of the potential consequences. Management accounting is, therefore, much more than just providing numerical analysis of costs and performance. It is about working with managers to run a sustainable business.

The T-Shaped Accountant

The Chartered Institute of Management Accountants (CIMA) put forward the idea of the T-shaped accountant, shown in Figure 11.1.

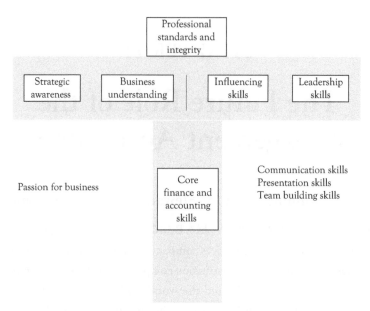

Figure 11.1 The T-shaped accountant

Today, the CIMA Forum describes the ideal form of the finance business partner as being a T-shaped accountant. By this they mean an accountant who has a core skill set of finance and accounting skills. Above this they should have a combination of skills which on the one side are about business understanding and strategic awareness and on the other, how to influence people and even provide leadership. This requires a passion for the business as well as the soft skill set. The T should be capped with professional standards to provide integrity. (CIMA 2009, p. 25)

In a study of management accounting in practice (Pitcher 2015) a finance director said that he didn't want his management accounting team sitting behind their desks in the office. "They should be out there in the business with the managers—that's when they are adding value." If the management accountant is to add value to the business they need to understand how the business works. The toolbox available to the management accountant does not just contain the accounting techniques, but also includes the strategy models and frameworks described in this book. Armed with this array of tools the management accountant is well placed to add significant value to the business. The management accountants should not be afraid to market their skills within the business. Managers are the customers of the management accountant and, once managers gain confidence in the abilities and advice received, the demand increases until the management accountant is part of the decision-making team.

There has been much written and talked about business partnering in which accountants work closely with the functional and business managers within the organization. The concept is actively promoted by accounting firms and consultants. Organizations have run internal programs titled "From Bookkeeping to Business Partnering" in order to develop better relationships with the business managers (Pitcher 2015). However, these are doomed to fail unless the accountant possesses the business knowledge as well as the accounting skills. McLellan (2014), in a study in the United States, noted the gap between the theory of management accounting and practice. Other studies have also noted that many practicing accountants tend to prefer and rely on the old tried and tested conventional techniques. Indeed these can be effective in supporting the strategic management process. It is important, however, that accounting bodies and education providers continue to develop the syllabus to ensure that the skill set is up to date and relevant to today's business environment. The recognition that accountants can make a valuable contribution to the strategic management process is being encapsulated in the definitions of management accounting by the professional bodies. As mentioned in Chapter 1, the Institute of Management Accountants (IMA) (2008, p. 1) definition includes the following phrases: "partnering in management decision making," and "to assist management in the formulation and implementation of an organization's strategy." The CIMA definition talks about providing information to generate and preserve value for organizations, and using a range of information, not just financial, to lead and inform business strategy and drive sustainable success. Therefore gone are the days when accountants were involved solely in the review and control activity. As demonstrated in this book the management accountant is able to contribute to every phase of the strategic management process. Armed with the techniques described and with the development of interpersonal skills, the management accountant will be able to provide influential insight, relevant information, and analysis that have impact, while building trust in relationships with managers to ensure high—caliber decision making to drive sustainable performance.

APPENDIX A

Strategic Management Accounting Techniques

1. Guilding, Cravens, and Tayles (2000) 2. Cadez (2006) 3. Cinquini and Tenucci (2007) 4. Cadez and Guilding (2008)					
Strategic management accounting (SMA) technique	Description	1	2	3	4
Activity-based costing	An approach to the costing and monitoring of activities, which involves tracing resources consumption and costing final outputs. Resources are assigned to activities and activities to cost objects based on consumption estimates. The latter utilize cost drivers to attach activity costs to outputs.			✓	
Attribute costing	An extension of activity-based costing using cost–benefit analysis (based on increased customer utility) to choose the product attribute enhancements that the company wants to integrate into a product.	✓	✓	✓	✓
Benchmarking	The establishment, through data gathering, of target and comparators, that permits relative levels of performance (and particularly areas of underperformance) to be identified. Adoption of identified best practices should improve performance.		✓	✓	✓
Brand value budgeting and monitoring	Brand valuation assigns financial value to the equity created by the name or image of a brand. It can be represented as the net present value of the estimated future cash flows attributable to the brand.	✓	✓		✓

Capital budgeting	The process of selecting long-term capital investments.		✓		
Competitor cost assessment	A technique in which the competitor cost per unit is attempted to be ascertained from available information. It is often at best an estimate.	✓	✓	✓	✓
Competitive position monitoring	Monitoring the market position and competitive strategy (market positioning) of the key competitors.	✓	✓	✓	✓
Competitor financial appraisal	Looking for strengths and weaknesses in the competitors' financial position.	✓	✓	✓	✓
Customer profitability analysis	CPA is the analysis of the revenue streams and service costs associated with specific customers or customer groups.		✓	✓	✓
Integrated performance measurement	The use of a range of performance measurement other than financial. The balanced scorecard is a typical example, which includes nonfinancial as well as financial, internal, and external measures, quantitative and qualitative. The balanced scorecard reviews performance from a number of different perspectives, for example, customer, internal business, and learning and growth as well as financial.		✓	✓	✓
Life cycle costing	Life cycle costing is the profiling of costs over the life of a product, including the preproduction stage.	✓	✓	✓	✓
Lifetime customer profitability analysis	Estimating the profitability of a customer over its lifetime taking into account future revenues and costs including cost of acquisition and retention.		✓		✓
Quality costing	The concept of quality costs is a means to quantify the total cost of quality-related efforts and deficiencies. It can be broken down into appraisal costs, prevention costs, and internal and external failure costs.	✓	✓	✓	✓
Strategic cost management	Strategic cost management is the overall recognition of the cost relationships among the activities in the value chain, and the process of managing those cost relationships to a firm's advantage.	✓	✓	✓	✓

Strategic pricing	Strategic pricing takes into account market segments, ability to pay, market conditions, competitor actions, trade margins, and input costs, as well as other potential factors affecting market position and demand for the product.	✓	✓	✓	✓
Target costing	Target costing is an activity that is aimed at reducing the life cycle costs of new products, by examining all possibilities for cost reduction at the research, development, and production stage. It is not a costing system, but a profit-planning system—the selling price and profit requirement are set during the research stage, thus creating a target cost.	✓	✓	✓	✓
Value chain costing	Based on Porter's value chain analysis, a firm may create a cost advantage either by reducing the cost of individual value chain activities or by reconfiguring the value chain. Once the value chain is defined, a cost analysis can be performed by assigning costs to the value chain activities.	✓	✓	✓	✓
Valuation of customers as assets	A technique similar to lifetime customer profitability that attempts to ascertain the net present value of a customer.	✓	✓	✓	✓

APPENDIX B

Income Statement and Balance Sheet for X Inc. and Y Inc.

Income statement for the year ended January 31, 20xx.

	X Inc.		Y Inc.	
	$000	$000	$000	$000
Revenue		4,000		6,000
Cost of sales				
Opening stock	200		800	
Purchases	3,200		4,800	
	3,400		5,600	
Less: closing stock	400		800	
		3,000		4,800
Gross profit		1,000		1,200
Expenses				
Distribution costs	200		150	
Administration expenses	290		250	
Total expense	_	490		400
Operating profit		510		800
Interest paid	_	10		400
Profit before tax		500		400
Taxation		120		90
Net profit for the period		380		310

Balance sheets as on January 31, 20xx

	X Inc. $000	X Inc. $000	Y Inc. $000	Y Inc. $000
Noncurrent assets				
Warehouse and office buildings	1,200		5,000	
Equipment and vehicles	600		1,000	
		1,800		6,000
Current assets				
Inventory	400		800	
Trade receivables	800		900	
Other receivables	150		80	
Cash and cash equivalents	—		100	
	1,350		1,880	
Less current liabilities				
Trade payables	800		800	
Other payables	80		100	
Short-term borrowing (overdraft)	200		—	
Current tax payable	120		90	
	1,200		990	
Net current assets		150		890
		1,950		6,890
Less long-term loan (10% p.a.)		—		4,000
Net assets		1,950		2,890

	$000	$000
Equity		
Share capital	1,000	1,600
Revaluation reserve	—	500
Retained profits	950	790
	1,950	2,890

References

Ansoff, I. 1965. *Corporate Strategy.* New York, NY: McGraw-Hill.

Atkinson, A.A., J.H. Waterhouse, and R.B. Wells. Spring, 1997. "A Stakeholder Approach to Strategic Performance Measurement." *Sloan Management Review* 38, no. 3, pp. 25–37.

Bromwich, M. 1988. "Managerial Accounting Definition and Scope—From a Managerial View." *Management Accounting* 66, no. 8, pp. 26–27.

Bryson, J. 2004. "What to Do When Stakeholders Matter: Stakeholder Identification and Analysis Techniques." *Public Management Review* 6, no. 1, pp. 29–30.

Cadez, S. 2006. "A Cross-Industry Comparative Analysis of Strategic Management Accounting Practices: An Exploratory Study." *Economic and Business Review for Central and South Eastern Europe* 8, no. 3, pp. 279–98.

Cadez, S., and C. Guilding. 2008. "An Exploratory Investigation of an Integrated Contingency Model of Strategic Management Accounting." *Accounting, Organizations and Society* 33, nos. 7–8, pp. 386–863.

Chartered Institute of Management Accountants. 2009. *Improving Decision Making in Organisations—The opportunity to reinvent finance business partners.* London: CIMA.

Cinquini, L., and A. Tenucci. 2007. "Is the Adoption of Strategic Management Accounting Techniques Really 'Strategy-Driven'? Evidence From a Survey." *Conference paper, Cost and Performance in Services and Operations,* Trento.

Clarkson, M.B.E. 1995. "A Stakeholder Framework for Analyzing and Evaluating Corporate Social Performance." *The Academy of Management Review* 20, no. 1, pp. 92–117.

Committee of Sponsoring Organizations of the Treadway Commission [COSO]. 2004. *Enterprise Risk Management—Integrated Framework: Application Techniques.* Durham, NC: American Institute of Certified Public Accountants.

Crane, A., and D. Matten. 2004. *Business Ethics.* Oxford, UK: Oxford University Press.

Davidson, H., W.J. Keegan, and E.A.Brill. 2003. *Offensive marketing: An action guide to gaining the offensive in business.* Abingdon. UK: Routledge.

Fitzgerald, L., R. Johnston, T.J. Brignall, R. Silvestro, and C. Voss. 1991. *Performance Measurement In Service Business.* London, UK: CIMA.

Freeman, R.E. 1984. *Strategic Management: A Stakeholder Approach.* Boston. MA: Pitman.

Govindarajan, V., and J.K. Shank. 1992. "Strategic Cost Management: Tailoring Controls to Strategies." *Journal of Cost Management* Fall 6, no. 3, pp. 14–24.

Guilding, C., K. Cravens, and M. Tayles. 2000. "An International Comparison of Strategic Management Accounting Practices." *Management Accounting Research* 11, no. 1, pp. 113–35.

Institute of Management Accountants. 2008. *Definition of Management Accounting, Statements of Management Accounting: Practice of Management Accounting.* Montvale, NJ: IMA.

Johnson, G., K. Scholes, and R. Whittington. 2007. *Exploring Corporate Strategy: Text and Cases,* 8th ed. Harlow, UK: Prentice Hall.

Kaplan, R. 1984. "The Evolution of Management Accounting." *The Accounting Review* 59, pp. 390–418.

Kaplan, R.S., and D.P. Norton. 1996. *The Balanced Scorecard.* Boston, MA: Harvard Business Review.

Langfield-Smith, K. 2008. "Strategic Management Accounting: How Far Have We Come in 25 years?" *Accounting, Auditing & Accountability Journal* 21, no. 2, pp. 204–28.

Lind, J., and T. Stromsten. 2006. "When do Firms Use Different Types of Customer Accounting?" *Journal of Business Research* 59, no. 12, pp. 1257–66.

Luhmann, N. 1996. "Modern Society Shocked By Its Risks." In *Social Sciences Research Centre occasional paper.* http://hub.hku.hk/handle/10722/42552 (accessed November 18, 2017).

McLellan, J.D. 2014. "Management Accounting Theory and Practice: Measuring the Gap in United States Businesses." *Journal of Accounting—Business and Management* 21, no. 1, pp. 53–68.

Mendelow, A. 1991. "Stakeholder Mapping." *Proceedings of the Second international Conference on Information Systems.* Cambridge, MA.

Mintzberg, H. 1999. "Who Should Control the Operation?" In *The Strategy Process,* eds. H. Mintzberg, J.B. Quinn, and S. Ghoshal. Harlow, UK: Pearson Education Ltd.

Mintzberg, H., and J.A. Waters. 1985. "Of Strategies, Deliberate and Emergent." *Strategic Management Journal* 6, no. 3, pp. 257–72.

Mitchell, R.K., B.R. Agle, and D.J. Wood. 1997. "Towards a Theory of Stakeholder Identification and Salience. Defining the Principle of Who and What Really Counts." *Academy of Management Review* 22, no. 4, pp. 853–86.

Nixon, B., and J. Burns. 2012. "The Paradox of Strategic Management Accounting." *Management Accounting Research* 23, no. 4, pp. 229–44.

Oboh, C.S., and S.O. Ajibolade. 2017. "Strategic Management Accounting and Decision Making: A Survey of the Nigerian Banks." *Future Business Journal* 3, no. 2, pp. 119–37.

Pitcher, G.S. 2015. "Management Accounting in Support of the Strategic Management Process." *CIMA Executive Summary Report* 11, no. 1. London: CIMA.

Porter, M.E. March-April, 1979. "How Competitive Forces Shape Strategy." *Harvard Business Review* 57, no. 2, pp. 137–45.

Porter, M.E. 1980. *Competitive Strategy, Techniques for Analysing Industries and Competition.* New York, NY: The Free Press.

Porter, M.E. 1985. *Competitive Advantage: Creating and Sustaining Superior Performance.* New York, NY: The Free Press.

Roslender, R., and S.J. Hart. 2003. "In search of Strategic Management Accounting: Theoretical and Field Study Perspectives." *Management Accounting Research* 14, no. 3, pp. 255–79.

Simmonds, K. 1981. "Strategic Management Accounting." *Management Accounting* 59, no. 4, pp. 26–9.

Simons, R. 1994. *Levers of Control.* New York, NY: McGraw-Hill.

Ward, K. 1992. *Strategic Management Accounting.* Oxford: Butterworth-Heinemann.

Whittington, R. 1996. "Strategy as Practice." *Long Range Planning* 29, no. 5, pp. 731–35.

About the Author

Graham S. Pitcher holds doctoral and masters level qualifications in business and education as well as being a qualified accountant. He is currently a consultant in professional and higher education and a senior lecturer at Nottingham Business School in the United Kingdom. Graham has 17 years practical experience as a management accountant and director working for organizations in manufacturing and direct marketing, as well as experience of both service and state sector organizations. Following a successful career as a practicing accounting in industry, Graham moved into professional education where he spent 14 years working with accountants, marketers, lawyers, and human resource professionals. He has held senior positions in private sector higher education institutions, such as the Dean of BPP Business School and Director of Business Education. He has worked extensively with the professional bodies in accounting, marketing, and HR, and has been involved in developing courses in a range of business-related subjects. He has written and published numerous articles on management accounting targeted at students and practitioners, and continues his research interests in management accounting in support of strategy.

Index

ABC. *See* Activity-based costing
ABM. *See* Activity-based management
Accounting rate of return, 127
Activity-based costing (ABC)
    benefits of, 97–98
    cost driver rate per activity, 96
    description of, 93–95
    overhead rate per product, 97
    process of, 96–97
    product information, 96
    selling price per product, 97
Activity-based management (ABM), 98–99
Adjusted market price, 158–159
After-sales service, 63
Appraisal, 99
Asset turnover, 71

Balanced scorecard, 144–147
Balance sheet, 183–184
Bargaining power
    of buyers, 25
    of suppliers, 25
Behavioral performance management, 165–166
Belief systems, 149
Benchmarking
    classification of, 162–163
    definition of, 161
    difficulties of, 162
    stages of exercise, 163–164
    uses and benefits of, 161–162
Boundary systems, 149
Build strategy, 41–42
Business environment
    changing, 15
    macro environment, 16–17
    task environment, 16–17
Business partnering, 138–139
Business risk, 129

Chartered Institute of Management Accountants (CIMA), 175–177
CIMA. *See* Chartered Institute of Management Accountants
Cluster analysis, 28–29
CLV. *See* Customer lifetime value
Competitive strategy
    activity-based costing, 93–98
    activity-based management, 98–99
    being stuck in the middle, 90–92
    cost implications of, 51–52
    cost leadership, 85–87
    costs of quality, 99–101
    differentiation, 87–88
    examples of, 90
    focus strategy, 88–89
    management accounting, 102
    value creation system, revisited, 92–93
Competitor analysis, 11
    cluster analysis, 28–29
    competitor information, 29–30
    competitor response profile, 29
    sources of competitor information, 31
Competitor information, 29–31
Competitor response profile, 29
Compliance, 175
Consolidation, 104–105
Consortia, 112
Corporate appraisal
    description of, 79–82
    GAP analysis, 82–84
    management accounting, 11–12, 84
    strategic management framework, 6–7
Corporate social responsibility (CSR), 171
Cost leadership, 85–87

Costs of quality, 99–101
Costs of quality report, 101
CPA. *See* Customer profitability analysis
Critical success factors, 147–148
CSR. *See* Corporate social responsibility
Currency risk, 161
Customer lifetime value (CLV), 59–60
Customer portfolio management, 60–62
Customer-positioning grid, 61
Customer profitability analysis (CPA)
    benefits of, 55–56
    costs to serve, 56–59
    customer lifetime value, 59–60
    description of, 54–55
Customers
    attitudes and behavior, 53–54
    financial performance of, 54
    history, 53
    identity, 53
    in organizations, 52
    value creation system, 62–67
Customer segment profitability analysis, 59

DELL value system, 65
De-merger, 113–114
Diagnostic use of control systems, 149
Differentiation, 87–88
Diversification, 105–106
Divest strategy, 43
Divisional performance, 149–152

Earnings per share (EPS), 75
ECIs. *See* Environmental condition indicators
Economic value added (EVA™)
    benefits, 154–155
    description of, 153–154
    drawbacks, 154–155
    key factors, 155–156
Emergent strategies, 9–10
Environmental analysis
    management accounting, 11, 31–34

strategic management framework, 5–6
    undertaking, 17–19
Environmental condition indicators (ECIs), 170
Environmental risk, 129
EVA™. *See* Economic value added
External failure, 99–100

Financial analysis
    asset turnover, 71
    earnings per share, 75
    gearing ratio, 72
    gross profit percentage, 69–70
    interest cover, 74–75
    inventory days, 74
    operating profit percentage, 70
    payables days, 74
    quick ratio, 73
    receivables days, 73–74
    return on capital employed, 70–71
    return on shareholders' funds or equity, 72
    working capital management, 72
    working capital ratio, 73
Financial controls and accounting techniques
    cash cows, 46
    dogs, 47
    question marks, 45–46
    rising stars, 46
Financial risk, 129
Focus strategy, 88–89
Formal strategic planning *vs.* emergent strategies, 9–10
Full manufacturing cost, 158
Full manufacturing cost plus, 158
Full market price, 158

GAP analysis, 82–84
Gearing ratio, 72
Gross profit percentage, 69–70
Growth vector matrix, 103

Harvest strategy, 42
Hold strategy, 42

IKEA value system, 65–66
Income statement, 183–184
Industry analysis
    bargaining power of buyers, 25
    bargaining power of suppliers, 25
    rivalry among existing competitors,
        26
    threat of new entrants or barriers to
        entry, 24–25
    threat of substitute products or
        services, 26
Institute of Management
        Accountants, 2
Integration issues, 112
Interactive use of control systems, 149
Interest cover, 74–75
Interlocking scorecards, 147–148
Internal appraisal
    9M's framework, 35–39
    customer profitability analysis,
        54–60
    financial analysis, 69–77
    management accounting, 11–12,
        77–78
    portfolio analysis, 40–48
    product life cycle, 48–52
    strategic management framework, 6
    supplier analysis, 67–68
    value creation system, 62–67
Internal failure, 99
Internal rate of return, 126–127
International markets, viable, 107
International risk, 129
Inventory days, 74
Inventory decisions, 50
Investment appraisal methods
    accounting rate of return, 127
    internal rate of return, 126–127
    net present value technique,
        125–126
    payback period, 124–125
    profitability index, 127
    real options, 127–128
Invest strategy, 41–42

Joint development forms
    consortia, 112
    de-merger, 113–114

joint venture, 112–113
    licensing, 113
    local agents, 113
    strategic alliance, 113
Joint venture, 112–113

Licensing, 113
Life cycle costing, 108–109
Lifetime customer profitability, 59
Linkages, industry sectors, 26–27
Local agents, 113

Machinery, 9M's framework, 37
Macro environment, 16–17
Makeup, 9M's framework, 37
Management, 9M's framework, 36
Management accountant, role of,
        175–177
Management accounting
    competitive strategies, 102
    corporate appraisal, 84
    definitions of, 1–2
    environmental analysis, 31–34
    internal appraisal, 11–12, 77–78
    performance management, 167
    strategic evaluation, 131–132
    strategic implementation, 133
    strategic options generation,
        114–116
    supporting strategic management
        process, 10–13
    sustainability, 171–173
Management information, 9M's
        framework, 38–39
Management performance indicators
        (MPIs), 170
Marginal cost, 157
Marginal cost plus, 158
Market development, 105
Market penetration, 103–104
Markets, 9M's framework, 37–38
Materials, 9M's framework, 38
Men and women, 9M's framework,
        35–36
Mergers and acquisitions, 110–111
Methods, 9M's framework, 37
Methods of growth
    integration issues, 112

mergers and acquisitions, 110–111
organic growth/internal
    development, 110
Money, 9M's framework, 36
MPIs. *See* Management performance
    indicators
Multidimensional performance
    measurement, 141–144

Negotiated price, 159
Net present value (NPV) technique,
    125–126
9M's framework, 35–39
Nokia, portfolio analysis, 47–48

Operating profit percentage, 70
Operational performance indicators
    (OPIs), 170
Operational risk, 129
OPIs. *See* Operational performance
    indicators
Opportunity cost, 159
Organic growth/internal
    development, 110

Payables days, 74
Payback period, 124–125
Performance management
    behavioral, 165–166
    management accounting, 167
Performance measurement
    multidimensional, 141–144
    in service organizations, 148–149
    traditional, 141
PESTEL framework
    economic factors, 21
    environmental factors, 23
    legal factors, 23
    political factors, 20
    sociocultural factors, 21–22
    technological factors, 22–23
PLC. *See* Product life cycle
Portfolio analysis
    axes, 40–41
    build/invest strategy, 41–42
    categorization and balanced
        portfolio, 41
    divest strategy, 43

drawbacks of, 44–45
harvest strategy, 42
hold strategy, 42
Nokia-case study, 47–48
uses of, 43–44
Prevention, 99
Pricing decisions, 50–51
Pricing policy, 106–107
Product development, 105
Product life cycle (PLC)
    accountant and, 50–52
    explanation of, 48–49
Profitability index, 127

Quick ratio, 73

Real options, 127–128
Receivables days, 73–74
Reputation risk, 129
Residual income (RI), 152–153
Resource audit, 35
Return on capital employed (ROCE),
    70–71
Return on investment (ROI),
    152–153
Return on shareholders' funds or
    equity, 72
Review and control
    management accounting, 13
    strategic management framework, 8
RI. *See* Residual income
Risk management
    definition of, 128–129
    process, 129–131
    types of risk, 129
ROCE. *See* Return on capital
    employed
ROI. *See* Return on investment

Sales and market life cycle, 49
Simons' levers of control, 149
Stakeholder analysis
    classification, 119
    connected stakeholders, 120
    definition of stakeholder, 118–119
    Dyson's decision, 122–123
    external stakeholders, 120–121
    internal stakeholders, 119–120

mapping, 121–122
Stewardship, 175
Strategic alliance, 113
Strategic evaluation
    elements of, 117
    financial evaluation, 123–124
    investment appraisal methods,
        124–128
    management accounting, 131–132
    risk management, 128–131
    stakeholder analysis, 118–123
Strategic implementation
    business partnering, 138–139
    changing needs of business, 137
    management accounting, 12–13,
        133
    operational budget, 133–135
    responsibility accounting, 136–137
    strategic management framework, 8
    tailoring accounting system,
        135–136
Strategic management, definition of,
    3–4
Strategic management accounting
    development of, 2–3
    techniques, 179–181
Strategic management framework
    corporate appraisal, 6–7
    environmental analysis, 5–6
    evaluation and choice, 7
    internal appraisal, 6
    mission and objectives, 5
    options generation, 7
    outlines of, 4
    review and control, 8
    strategic implementation, 8
Strategic options generation
    consolidation, 104–105
    diversification, 105–106
    growth methods, 109–112
    growth vector matrix, 103
    international markets, 107
    joint development forms, 112–114

life cycle costing, 108–109
    management accounting, 12,
        114–116
    market development, 105
    market penetration, 103–104
    mix of options, 106
    pricing policy, 106-107
    product development, 105
    strategic management framework, 7
    target costing, 108
    withdrawal, 103
Strategy formulation, 8–9
Supplier analysis, 67–68
Supplier appraisal, 67
Supplier approval, 67
Supplier rating, 67–68
Sustainability
    definition of, 169
    management accounting, 171–173
    reasons for, 169–170
    reporting, monitoring, and control,
        170–171
Sustainable development, 169
SWOT analysis, 79–82

Target costing, 108
Task environment, 16–17
Tax regimes, 160
Traditional performance
        measurement, 141
Transfer pricing
    across international borders,
        159–161
    in divisional performance, 156–157
    options for, 157–159
T-shaped accountant, 175–177

Value creation system, 62–67
    revisited, 92–93

Withdrawal, 103
Working capital management, 72
Working capital ratio, 73

OTHER TITLES IN THE MANAGERIAL ACCOUNTING COLLECTION

Kenneth A. Merchant, University of Southern California, Editor

- *Revenue Management: A Path to Increased Profits, Second Edition* by Ronald J. Huefner
- *Cents of Mission: Using Cost Management and Control to Accomplish Your Goal* by Dale R. Geiger
- *Sustainability Reporting: Getting Started, Second Edition* by Gwendolen B. White
- *Lies, Damned Lies, and Cost Accounting: How Capacity Management Enables Improved Cost and Cash Flow Management* by Reginald Tomas Lee, Sr.
- *Strategic Management Accounting: Delivering Value in a Changing Business Environment Through Integrated Reporting* by Sean Stein Smith

Announcing the Business Expert Press Digital Library

Concise e-books business students need for classroom and research

This book can also be purchased in an e-book collection by your library as

- a one-time purchase,
- that is owned forever,
- allows for simultaneous readers,
- has no restrictions on printing, and
- can be downloaded as PDFs from within the library community.

Our digital library collections are a great solution to beat the rising cost of textbooks. E-books can be loaded into their course management systems or onto students' e-book readers.

The **Business Expert Press** digital libraries are very affordable, with no obligation to buy in future years. For more information, please visit **www.businessexpertpress.com/librarians**. To set up a trial in the United States, please email **sales@businessexpertpress.com**.